A Taste

Recipes and

This is a factual account of my early life and of my experiences whilst taking part in the Great British Bakeoff. Some names have been changed to protect the innocent (and the guilty).

This book is dedicated to my wife Iris in recognition of her support and patience during my Bakeoff experience. I would also like to acknowledge the valuable help given by my daughter Corinne who lent her food styling expertise and photographic skills to the majority of the photographs.

Finally, a very special thanks to my colleague at Strathisla Visitor Centre, Michael Collins, for contributing his editorial skills.

PublishNation

www.publishnation.co.uk

Table of Contents

CHAPTER ONE

To The Far Side of The World

Meatball Curry

CHAPTER TWO

Portknockie Welcomes Norman

MINCE 'n TATTIES

CHAPTER THREE Applying for The Bakeoff

JALOUSIE aux POMMES

CHAPTER FOUR

Off to School

SCOTCH BROTH with BOILED SILVERSIDE

CHAPTER FIVE

The Recipes

BLACK FOREST SWISS ROLL Mk.I

Almond & Raspberry Fresh Cream Cakes

THE RESEARCH

GARIBALDI SCONES

CHAPTER SIX – 1954

When I was Seven

LENTIL & CARROT SOUP

WHOLEMEAL BLOOMER

CHAPTER SEVEN

More Recipes

Orange and Raspberry Savarin Yeasted Cake

The Dobos Torte MkI

Orange & Raspberry Savarin Cake

CHAPTER EIGHT

Now Eight I Join The Cubs

Norman's Scottish Tablet

CHAPTER NINE

Off To The Tent

Cheese Souffle

CHAPTER TEN

Now Cooking At School

Chinese Wedding Cake

CHAPTER ELEVEN

The Bakeoff Week Two – Biscuits

Chicken Tarragon and Mushroom Pie

CHAPTER TWELVE

To Aberdeen Wireless College

Cheese Scones

CHAPTER THIRTEEN

Week Three of The Bakeoff - Bread

PEAR & FRANGIPANE TARTS

CHAPTER FOURTEEN

To Mrs Murphy's in East Ham

Prawn Foo Yung

CHAPTER FIFTEEN

Week Four of The Bakeoff – Puddings

Lemon Meringue Pie

CHAPTER SIXTEEN

Bound for The Orient

Shortbread Biscuits

CHAPTER SEVENTEEN

Week Five of The Bakeoff – Pies

The Pieffel Tower

Vegetarian Nut Roast Wellington

CHAPTER EIGHTEEN

The Final of The Bakeoff & The Extra Slice

FARTHING BISCUITS

CHAPTER NINETEEN

Frequently Asked Questions

CHAPTER ONE

To The Far Side of The World

In December 1965, the Staff Clerk at the Marconi Marine depot in Liverpool allocated me three weeks leave, after which I was to travel to the Depot in Tiger Bay, Cardiff for a radar maintenance course. They had booked me into the Merchant Navy Hotel in Cardiff for the duration of the course. I just had to get myself there, no easy matter by train. I think today that I would have travelled from Aberdeen to London, then on to Cardiff via the G.W.R. As it turned out, I caught the train for Glasgow then Crewe where I spent about 6 hours due to delays, arriving in Cardiff at five am, very tired. I waited near the station café until it opened at six am, all the time having to listen to a budding Tom Jones singing as he loaded newspapers into a van. Most of the Welsh think they can sing, although this chap was not too bad, he might have been a refugee from a male voice choir. I had a morning cup of coffee before deciding I had better try to find the hotel.

Once I found the hotel, it had not opened for the day and no one appeared to have heard me ringing the doorbell. I was still sitting on my suitcase at seven am when the doors opened. After meeting some of the others taking the same course, we boarded a cab for the Marconi Depot near the docks in Tiger Bay. I met the rest of the attendees, there were eight of us in total, all there to learn about the Marconi Radiolocator Mark IVB with True Motion. During the day, we were introduced to magnetrons, microwaves, klystrons, wave-guide extenders and listened to numerous tales of the sea from our instructor Emlyn Beam Tetrode an ex Radio Officer himself, who decided he had seen enough salt water and hung up his sea boots.

The nights were the best part of the radar course, it was back to the hotel, into the bar and then dinner before going out on the town. Cardiff was indeed a good run ashore and we frequently ended our evenings in a Chinese restaurant before heading back for some kip and another exciting day in Tiger Bay. Weekends found us at the Top Rank Dancing in Castle Street where there appeared to be a great abundance of "talent". I discovered much later that two of the lads on the course had married young ladies they met in Cardiff, but I was far too young for that caper; one found his girl with child and had to do the honourable thing, the other suffered a blow on the head from a radar scanner. I did have a few dates whilst I was there but no lasting friendships. Before I went to sea, my Mam found it necessary to advise me to "watch myself" whilst away from home, she believed I should "save myself" for when I fell in love. I asked how I would know when I fell in love, she said when you do fall in love, there will be a flash of lightning and a clap of thunder. To date I have never seen the flash but quite often had the clap!

Full of beer, cider and Chinese food we completed the course in four short weeks and I boarded a train bound for Liverpool, all ready to sign on as Radio Officer on the MV Weirbank, a tramp steamer belonging to the Bank Line of Glasgow. After getting off the train in Liverpool Lime Street, I took a cab to Bootle then to the Langton Dock where I found my ship, the Weirbank, registered in Glasgow and very smart she looked too. The Weirbank was a relatively new addition to the Bank Line Fleet of over seventy ships. Built in 1961 she was 6,354 tonnes, had fifty-seven Indian crew and sixteen white men on articles plus yours truly, Marconi Sahib. She looked in superb condition and all ready to set sail for the Gulf of Mexico and other distant shores. This was to be a six-month long trip but nonetheless we all signed two year foreign going articles. The Master and Commander was Captain Jack Reid, a genial Geordie with a great love for curry, he was in the right place as the Indian galley staff produced a curry for lunch and dinner every day. Coming from Portknockie I had never seen a curry before never mind eaten one. All that was to change and before six months was up I had eaten just about anything you could name in a curry. Unlike the stuff we get from Indian carryout shops these days, I never had anything whilst on board the Weirbank which was over-spicy, Capt. Jack saw to that, every curry had to be just the way he liked it, otherwise the Chief Steward was called to the saloon for interrogation, especially if it was too hot.

MV Weirbank

Once we had dropped off the pilot at the Liverpool Bar, we were underway and setting a westerly course, bound for the United States of America. We had a cargo of bricks on board for the Grand City Hall in New York then it was south to Charleston in South Carolina. Next stop was Savannah in Georgia before rounding the Florida peninsula enroute for Mobile Alabama. In Mobile we loaded earth moving equipment for Australia before docking in New Orleans where I sampled a Poor Boy sandwich, the like of which I'd never seen before. This sandwich was about a foot long and packed with roast beef, cheese and salad. The cost was one dollar U.S., and I shared it with one of the deck apprentices, as I would have found it difficult to eat the whole thing on my own. Among other stuff we loaded in New Orleans were two hundred cases of Bacardi Rum, which was locked away in our special cargo locker. Next stop in the Gulf was Galveston, loading machinery for South Australia. Finally, we called in to a place I had never heard of, Brownsville in Texas. We took a trip ashore and visited one of the few bars in the dockside area; they had a country and western band playing there. They played a lot of the Maw 'n Paw an' the dog died kind of stuff and that was the first time I heard that famous country song, "I'd rather have a bottle in front o' me, than a frontal lobotomy." Later we ordered a pizza pie between us and when it arrived, it was on a tray around two feet in diameter and we all had one slice each except for the second engineer who had two slices, but then he had paid for it. I quite enjoyed it, it was superior to anything you can buy in the UK these days and of course much bigger but this was the USA after all. That was the first time I had eaten a pizza, I was beginning to lead a very exotic life; curry and pizza, what next?

After our transit of the Panama Canal, we again set a westerly course taking the Bank Line Sunshine Route for Brisbane in Australia. We travelled at economy speed and it took us thirty-two days to reach Brisbane, seldom seeing another ship and making no landfall on the way. Today Brisbane is a bit hazy in my memory, the only feature I can recall is the heat, I think it was around thirty degrees centigrade when we first went ashore in Brisbane and I can remember being in a tram at one stage. We discharged a few bits of earthmoving equipment before sailing for Sydney.

Sydney was all you would expect of a large city and as soon as we had docked, we had the shore-side telephone installed in the ship's office. We were to be in Sydney for around a week and the phone was required for contacting the ship's agent and other business. The first call we received however was from a nurse at one of Sydney's hospitals, asking if we would like to organise a party, as there were a large number of expat nursing staff employed at the hospital looking forward to meeting folks from home. Apparently, this was normal practice for Sydney and other Australian ports. The nurses had contacts within the telephone company and calls from the hospital were normally among the first received by most ships. I think we had two parties on board the Weirbank in Sydney. We supplied the beer, of course. The stuff we were drinking in Sydney was Foster's Lager, bought from the off-licence near the dock gates and wrapped up in newspaper to keep it cool on the way back to the ship. We also attended a beach barbecue organised by one of the hospitals, I seem to remember it was at Manly Beach. We had brought along some beer and a few bottles of Bacardi Rum, salvaged from the special cargo "breakages". Unfortunately, an oversupply of males turned up for the party, mainly Greeks who drank all the Bacardi.

One of the must visit places in Sydney was the famous Bondi beach, this was pre Opera House days and the only significant landmark was Sydney Harbour Bridge, recognisable worldwide.

Bondi was very hot and although there were large numbers of sunbathers we did not join them, we just had a swim in the surf before heading for the shade and a cold beer or two. We spotted quite a few lifeguards on the beach whose skin was very dark; they are probably all dead now from skin cancer. Nowadays, of course, Bruce and Sheila do the "Slip-Slop-Slap" routine before heading out in the sun. Bondi was the birthplace of the famous "Bondi Wave" – nothing to do with surf but was the movement of your hand in front of your face in an attempt to wave away the flies. You really do need a hat with corks hanging from it if you plan to visit Aussie, although the midges on the west coast of Scotland come a close second to the Australian fly for nuisance value. It was while we were in Sydney that one of the dockers explained to us the difference between Australian men and Australian women – the women can spit further!

A week after docking in Sydney we were sailing up the Yarra River and tying up alongside in Melbourne Victoria. You will appreciate how long ago this was when I tell you that the pubs were still closing at 6pm and Australia was still using £A's as currency. Once we were alongside I set out for the local Marconi Marine Office, running short of drinking vouchers, I needed a salary advance and a top-up of Aussie pounds would suit me fine. Outside the dock gates, I spoke to a policeman to ask for directions, he was wearing a pith helmet to guard against the heat. I could have done with the helmet myself as I was feeling the heat on my head but thought it best not to pinch his hat, I may get accused of taking the pith!. We were on the other side of the World here in Melbourne and this copper was the first "native" I had spoken to in Victoria. His accent sounded familiar and I asked where he came from; he answered Cornhill, Banffshire, which is around fifteen miles from my own place of birth, Portknockie. The World was getting smaller! Most people when asked would say that Scotland's biggest export is Scotch whisky, that is not true, it is still Scotsmen. One of Melbourne's highlights for us was Mabel's Pie Shop, located in a railway arch just outside the dock gates, selling pie beans and chips for half a crown. Having existed mainly on curry for a few months, pie and chips was a welcome change.

Leaving Melbourne behind we had a short stop at Adelaide before our final port of call in Australia, Port Pirie where we spent a couple of days loading lead ingots for the UK. Ore smelting was the main industry in Port Pirie. Port Pirie illustrated to us in 1966 just how young a country Australia really was. The main street was unmetalled, just a dry dusty strip with boardwalk style walkways along the fronts of the buildings. The Lone Ranger would not have felt out of place there. He would probably have found a silver mine quite nearby if he needed some new bullets. Port Pirie was our final discharge port as well as being where we loaded our first homeward bound cargo, the lead. As we were equipped with six deep tanks for the transport of coconut oil, that was to be our final cargo, loading at Rabaul, New Britain before heading for the UK and Liverpool. First we had to load copra which is the inside part of the coconut, this was to form the bulk of our cargo. The copra was not however all located in one place, we had to do a tour of the Pacific picking up a little here and there. Some of these islands had no harbour to speak of and most times we dropped the hook and had our stern line made fast round a palm tree on shore.

I think we were very privileged in visiting these remote locations in the sixties, most likely we had managed to visit many places that had escaped the attention of David Attenborough in his Zoo Quest days. Our tour of the Pacific included the following islands, Noumea, New Caledonia, Port Moresby, Lae, Kawieng, Honiara in the Solomons, and Nauru among others. We even visited the island of Vanua Lava to the north of Vanuatu. This island is where the Hesperus was wrecked at the turn of last century. The Hesperus was carrying as cargo a complete circus from Germany to Australia and unfortunately shipwrecked on the island. Sadly, the survivors were attacked and killed by the cannibal natives of the island. One day, two of the natives were eating a clown when one turns to the other and says; "Does this taste funny to you?" Our final loading port was Rabaul in New Britain where, in addition to a large cargo of copra we loaded the coconut oil. I can easily remember the dates we were in Rabaul as it included Anzac Day 1966, April 25th.

The only bar ashore in Rabaul was the Rabaul Yacht Club, and all Bank Line personnel, together with all members of the British Royal Navy, were honorary members. The day prior to Anzac day two British Royal Navy submarines had docked in Rabaul. Contingents from both these submarines joined the crew of the Weirbank for the Anzac Day parade. Unfortunately, during the parade, some of the off-duty submarine crews had found their way to the yacht club and after getting tanked up had started a fight. They had to get the police to the club to sort it out and of course had to disrupt the Anzac Day parade to get the job done. Had it not been Anzac day when we were in Rabaul it is unlikely I would have remembered being there at all.

The only other memory I have from Rabaul is the rain. At around 2pm every afternoon the heavens opened and for around an hour we had a tropical downpour. Whilst it was chucking it down all loading work ceased and the hundred or so natives employed to load the sacks of copra took shelter under the canvas deck shelters. I regret that one thing, not having a tape recorder with me, as the native workers would start to sing. It was an amazing sound and far superior to anything I had ever heard before, might even have given the Welsh a run for their money. They sang in their own language so it was unintelligible to us, although very melodic. The other language in use throughout these Pacific Islands was Pidgin English. Pidgin in the islands even had its own newspaper, The Nu Gini Tok Tok. The native workers had little use for money and most of their wages was in the form of food and tobacco. They used to roll the tobacco up in newspapers into a giant cigar. For this purpose, they were also given newspapers along with the tobacco; normally The South Pacific Post which, at one time was listed in the Guinness Book of Records as "The most smoked newspaper in the World".

The majority of the natives in Rabaul had extended holes in their ear lobes as far as being able to pass a golf ball through the loop and some were even bigger. So that these lobes would not be caught in anything during the working day, they used to loop them over the top of the ear, not the most attractive of sights. I notice some of the citizens in the UK starting to disfigure their ears in the same manner. In fact at the first Bakeoff audition I attended in Manchester there was one budding contestant who had one ear done in a similar fashion with an inserted ring around 2" diameter. I thought to myself "He's gonna be good at the doughrings". The first European sailors to return home sporting tattoos had them done in the South Seas; it is no surprise then to find us going the same way with the ears. I still count myself as being fortunate in that I never got so drunk as to blindly subject myself to the tattooist's needle. I am not saying I am anti-tattooing; in fact, some of them are extremely artistic and nice to look at, at least when you are still young. When gravity takes control in later years, most people probably have second thoughts about body art.

Eventually we were fully loaded with copra and coconut oil and headed west again, at around 12 knots we expected to take around forty days to reach Liverpool. We would have a brief stop in Aden for bunkers then north through the Suez Canal. I think it was once we had cleared Port Said and sailed into the Mediterranean that all the copra bugs died. These are wee beasties that accompany the cargo of copra and they cover the whole ship, playing hell with the Mate's painting programme. Once you enter colder climes, they all die and things get back to normal. The one good thing is that they do not bite. We managed to make the Bar at Liverpool and picked up the pilot forty-one days after leaving Rabaul. It was cold and misty with a fine drizzle in the night air but the smell of home, coupled with the faint whiff of frying from the chippie at Birkenhead, was a joy, having been away for six months and ten days. The next day we signed off articles and I was off to the Marconi Marine depot in Liverpool to see how much leave they were going to let me have, then it was a train journey north.

I was home for three weeks so I bought my first car, a 1953 Ford Popular for £20 and a further £9-10/- for third party fire and theft insurance. I could not however envisage anyone wanting to steal it. The car only had three gears and a maximum speed of around 45 mph but it was great fun. Perhaps I managed to survive my teenage years because it would only reach top speed when going downhill.

One of my favourite curries whilst serving on the Weirbank was Kofta Curry, I was given the recipe by the Deck Serang (Bosun) on board. He had obtained the recipe from the cook and gave me a translation. I have made this meatball curry dozens of times in the past forty years, including first of all making it for Mam and Dad. I tracked down most of the spices and ingredients and proudly served it to them one Saturday evening with a boiled rice accompaniment. It took me two or three days to eat it all myself as my parents would not touch it and Mam said it took her days to get rid of the smell in the kitchen. How times have changed, with most of the British population thinking nothing of buying an Indian at the weekend. I always make my own curry as I think most of the Indian restaurants in this country are nowhere near being able to produce the genuine article, most of them having three buckets of sauce in the kitchen - mild, medium and hot. You will be saying that if you are making Kofta Curry you should use lamb; however, my recipe uses beef; eating lamb where I come from is akin to cannibalism.

That trip on the Weirbank marked a high point in my initial career at sea, my first trip in charge and a circumnavigation of the World to boot and still only eighteen. I wasn't quite sure where to make a start on the story of my Bakeoff experience but finally decided that I would go back, start at the beginning and weave a tale using my early life and the weeks I spent on the Bakeoff. Before I take you back to the Portknockie of 1947 I will let you have my recipe for Meatball Curry, if all you get out of this book is this recipe, then you will have done well.

The meatball curry I make now uses low fat minced steak; 250g making sixteen meatballs and with the spices and other ingredients, together with boiled rice and/or naan will feed four people easily. I have included the recipe here, although it is probably nothing like the original one I brought home from the Weirbank. I have also included a recipe for naan, which I bake under the grill but ideally, it should be done in a tandoor oven. By the way, I would like to offer my apologies to one of my fellow Bakeoff contestants and good friend Chetna, as this is about as far away from The Cardigan Trail as you can get! So hold on to your bindi Chets, this may cause some hilarity in the Punjab. Bon appetit.

Meatball Curry

Ingredients

The Meatballs

250g finest minced steak

½ onion finely chopped

1 garlic clove minced

½ tsp salt

1 tsp Garam Masala

1 green chilli deseeded and chopped finely

1 tbsp tomato puree

1 tsp ground coriander

½ tsp turmeric

2 tbsps oil

1 beaten egg

The Curry Sauce

½ onion sliced

2 tbsp vegetable oil

2 cloves garlic minced

1 red chilli, deseeded and finely chopped

1 tsp cumin

1 pce ginger 1" long, peeled and finely grated

 Tsp chilli flakes

1 tbsp tomato puree

½ tsp salt

½ dessert apple finely chopped

3 tbsp orange juice

200ml stock beef or chicken

The Naan

150g strong flour

5g active dried yeast

1 tsp salt

20ml olive oil

90ml water

Method

The Meatballs

Place all ingredients in a food processor and mix well before transferring to a well-floured work surface. Alternatively, you can mix by hand in a large bowl. Divide into 16 pieces and roll each piece into a ball using flour to prevent sticking. Add two tablespoons vegetable oil to a hot frying pan and brown the meatballs before removing to a plate whilst you prepare the sauce.

The Curry Sauce

Add two tablespoons vegetable oil to a hot pan and fry the onion and garlic before adding the chilli flakes and red chilli, cumin, ginger and tomato puree, frying for two minutes. Add the salt, apple, orange juice and stock. Then add the browned meatballs, stir well and simmer for one hour. Taste and season as required.

The Naan

Mix all ingredients and knead for ten minutes before placing in a bowl, cover with a damp cloth and leave for one hour. After one hour, the dough should be doubled in size. Divide the dough in four and roll each piece out to whatever shape you require your naans to be. Place on a baking tray, cover and leave for 30 minutes or so. When you are ready to serve the curry, spray the naan with oil and place under a hot grill until risen and browned before turning and repeating on the other side. Serve immediately with the curry and boiled rice.

Note: I usually include a slack handful of sultanas when I add the stock but this is not everyone's choice so I sometimes leave them out.

Another addition we have with curry but only with the meatball one is a hardboiled egg, don't ask me why but I think we may have inherited this from my brother-in-law Stanley Bowie, who himself had spent 3 years with the Bank Line and was a curry aficionado. He always blamed his stomach ulcer on the Bank line food, an excess of spices perhaps, rather than my sister's cooking as she was an excellent chef.

CHAPTER TWO

Portknockie Welcomes Norman

The war had been over for two years and in a few months, India was to gain her independence from the United Kingdom. It was the evening of midsummer's day and still daylight; the Mavis was singing his song from the rooftops when the baker left home just after ten o'clock. He was heading for the home of Mrs Henderson; the time had come for her to do her work. Mrs Henderson was the wife of Jock Henderson, the signalman at Portknockie Railway Station and part-time handyman. Mrs Henderson was also quite a handy person, she was about to drag screaming into the world Portknockie's latest recipient of National Dried Milk and orange juice.

It was just past midnight when Norman Calder was born, missing the longest day of the year by around ten minutes. Most women would agree however that any day a child is born feels like the longest day! Mrs Henderson earned her five shillings that day and as the father ran one of the local bakeries, she got a loaf of bread and half a dozen softies. As this was a Sunday, it was not until the Monday morning at six o'clock that the baker carried a white bundle into the bakery, to introduce all seven pounds eight ounces of his new son to the other bakers as Norman, a wee brother for Ian and Sybil. Apparently he was a bit of a showstopper then as all work in the bakery ceased for around 3 minutes (that by the way is a long time for a baker to stand and do nothing - ask Paul Hollywood or Davie Findlay). After a quick baptism of rice flour, the newly born was returned to the bottom drawer of the tallboy.

That was the start of my life. A great deal has happened since then; India has retained her independence and echoed Scotland in sending her citizens all over the world. India has done rather well for herself but my own life and career has not been quite so successful. Perhaps I have tried too many different things but have had no particularly outstanding achievements; I would say if there is a talent within me at all, it is in not being afraid to try something new or different. As you will see, I will have a go at just about anything. If I had to classify myself and my life I'd put myself down as a bit of a rolling stone, gathering little moss but as someone said to me once, you may gather no moss as a rolling stone but you do get polished. Well maybe, but it is difficult to act as your own judge on that, the only visible, polished part of me that I am aware of is the top of my head, where the hair was once wavy but eventually waved itself goodbye.

Eighteen months later, my Mam called once more upon the services of Mrs Henderson, to assist my new brother Robert into the world. As a token of gratitude to Mrs. Henderson, Robert was given an additional name, a middle name if you like and that was Henderson. He has, however, always been called Robert (among other things) but never to my knowledge has he been called Henderson. Despite the tendency of some middle class families in the UK to give their sons Scottish surnames as Christian names, I cannot recall anyone being given the first name of Henderson. Apart from "Hen Broon " of the Broons in the Sunday Post who may well have originally been called "Henderson Broon", but I'm not too sure about that, we'd need to get in touch with DC Thompson in Dundee to find out for sure. The middle name of George had also been included on my own birth certificate. This was possibly a nod to the reigning monarch but it could well have been after my great grandfather, Geordie Stephen, who knows, I should have asked Mam, but we are all guilty of not learning enough from our parents or not asking them enough relevant questions about their own upbringing. This was my motivation for getting the details of my life down on paper; I felt it important to ensure that the generations following are not sitting wondering who we were and what we did. It was a good thing my birth did not occur after 1952, otherwise I may have been called Elizabeth. Life is fortunate at times.

No memory exists in my mind of my short stay at 8 Park Street, as we moved to a bigger house in 1948 but it was still in Portknockie. The house was called Summerton and this is where Robert was born. He cost more than me as Mrs. Henderson had to walk twice as far now that we'd moved, my mother had to part with 7/6d for Robert. Mam said he should have cost less as he was a smaller baby than I had been but just by a few ounces; this may have been due to the cigarettes she'd started smoking to help relieve the trauma of working in the bakery and having me to look after as well as my older brother Ian and sister Sybil. Summerton had been the name of a herring drifter which was part owned by Joseph Addison, who had built Summerton in 1906. Which came first I'm not certain but it's possible he had built the house Summerton from the profits of the herring industry, as was the case for most of the grand houses built along the Moray Firth coast in the late 19th/early 20th century.

Summerton was a very large property, one of the bigger ones in Portknockie, with six bedrooms and a large kitchen where we lived most of the time as it had a Rayburn stove and it was normally quite warm. With no central heating the rest of the house was a wee bit hill billy. In the kitchen there was a bell response indicator which had six little windows behind which a coloured disc would vibrate to indicate the particular room which was calling. Presumably, this was installed in the days when people had servants. The rooms which had a bell-push on the wall were; the Drawing Room, Lounge, Dining Room, Bedroom One and Bedroom Two. As wee boys Robert and I used to ring these bells quite often, but no one ever responded, apart from my Dad who would say, "Ring that bell again and ye'll get a fat lug". That was one of my Dad's favourite threats, although fortunately for us, the threat was never carried out.

Summerton was an enormous house and so big that my Mam had to employ a lady to help with looking after the place, assisting with the cooking and cleaning and perhaps more importantly she helped look after me and Robert. Part of the job description for looking after us was taking Robert out for a walk in the pram. This was fine for Robert in the pram, unfortunately for me, I had to walk and even more unfortunately, Winnie, for that was the name of the lady, also liked walking, but I would add - with a vengeance. The next village to Portknockie was Finechty, approximately two miles distant and there was nothing that Winnie liked more than a walk to Finechty, call in past Uncle Wullie's and back to Portknockie. A four mile trot for a three year old was a fair distance and appeared to be even longer with me having to listen to Winnie humming highland pipe tunes on the way, interspersed with the occasional hymn. Perhaps that is why I have rather perversely been fond of walking ever since, although my present attack of plantar fasciitis has poleaxed that part of my recreational life for the moment. From my place of birth at number 8 Park Street it is not far to walk to the War Memorial which was erected in memory of the inordinate amount of soldiers, sailors, airmen and citizens of Portknockie who gave their lives in the Great War and the Second World War.

From the War Memorial head west along Church Street and turn right at the Kirk then proceed down the Bakers Brae. It was called The Bakers Brae for obvious reasons, it was where Alicky Baker had his bakery & shop. It was also one of the best streets in Portknockie for sledging in the wintertime, in fact it was possible to mount your sledge at the top of Hill Street (where the railway line was) and go down the Bakers Brae then all the way to the harbour without stopping. A good friend of mine, Frank Slater, accomplished this feat many times but that was before there were many cars about; when he was a youngster there were perhaps only two or three cars in the village. After going down the brae, walk just past the old Post office and you'll see a small cottage with its gable end facing the Moray Firth. When I was a bairn this was the home of my great Aunt Hepzibah Robb or Auntie Heppy as we called her. My Granda always said she was Robb by name and Robb by nature, which on reflection was a bit unfair as she was in fact quite a generous soul. She once returned from holiday with a large tin box of Pontefract Cakes which she had mistakenly bought thinking they were cakes. Turned out they were liquorice buttons, which Robert and I got a few of every time we visited her, this was in fact every day until the tin was empty. Auntie Heppy had been a nursing officer with the British Army in India and settled in Portknockie after her retirement. Heppy was very well spoken and took the time to teach us good manners and to try to get us to speak correctly. One of my particular memories is of Heppy emphasizing that a reef was a type of knot or a structure you would find made of coral in the Pacific Ocean, rather than the ceiling or the roof of the house.

Auntie Heppy later departed this earth from my Granny's spare bedroom at 8 Park Street. This had been the location of my birth in 1947, although there's no blue plaque there yet! The spare bedroom at 8 Park Street was where Robert and I had to sleep whenever our parents went away for a wee holiday (thankfully not too often). It was a creepy place before Auntie Heppy's demise but even worse after that, as we had to sleep in the bed she had died

21

in and I'm not sure if my Granny had bothered to change the sheets; perhaps she had and it was just our imagination that made the whole experience worse than it need have been. The situation wasn't improved either by the presence of a large painting hanging on the wall at the end of the bed. This painting, or perhaps it was a print, was of an angel carrying the body of a small child in her arms up to heaven; this style of painting was very popular in Victorian times, what with so many children dying in infancy. Never did take to it myself – the angel had a smile on her face. We believed in angels in those days. We always fell asleep at Granny's smelling of carbolic soap and with the vision of an angel in our minds. Angels were something else we were told about as children which turned out to be another fairy tale; angels, like the unicorn, never existed, experiments have shown that the breastbone would have to extend forward over 48" in order to provide enough anchorage for the huge amount of muscles and ligaments necessary to get the wings flapping.

It is worth mentioning my Auntie Heppy because of her and my own connection to Tomintoul. The village of Tomintoul is not very well known outside, well Tomintoul. It is perhaps best known to children at school as the highest village in the Highlands and to others for its connection to Percy Toplis (The Monocled Mutineer). George Greig, the Tomintoul local bobby in 1920, was shot in the shoulder by Toplis, who was a murderer on the run and who'd taken refuge in a local farmer's bothy. The farmer concerned had alerted the bobby and he was also shot. Fortunately, both survived. Toplis was later shot and killed by the police near Penrith on 6th June 1920. My own connection to Tomintoul is a photograph taken in 1950 of me being held up in front of a cast iron fountain in Tomintoul village square. The other person in the photograph was Great Aunt Hepzibah. The occasion hasn't been remembered by me but I do remember Aunt Hepzibah. In the photo she is wearing a dead fox round her neck, which was fashionable around the time of the Great War; she had several of them in her wardrobe which we found fascinating.

The dead foxes aside, it looks like Heppy was fond of animals, as when she had returned from India, she'd brought a vast collection of elephants with her – but these were small ones, carved from ivory and ebony. They were considered extremely unlucky and when Mam inherited them on Heppy's death, she gave them to the jumble sale. Today in Portknockie and indeed other places round the northeast of Scotland, elephants are still regarded superstitiously as being unlucky unless one keeps their trunks pointed toward the door. Personally, just to be on the safe side I wouldn't have an elephant or rather a model or stuffed elephant indoors under any circumstances.

Although unable to recall being in Tomintoul in 1950 there are memories of the summer of that year. At three years old, Robert and me were let loose on the lawn with the baby bath filled with water one hot summer day and we had a splash in the garden. My recollections are that a photograph of this occasion exists but it has not been seen for years. It wasn't many days after that hot summer afternoon when we found the jar of boiled sweets in the bottom of the dining room store cupboard. That was human error, why on earth did some-one put the jar in the bottom of the cupboard when there may have been space at the top, away from our curious eyes. In any case Robert and me left the dining room with a pocketful each of hard sugary boiled sweets. I managed the first one OK but Robert choked on his one. Fortunately, Winnie was passing through the hallway and realised something was amiss. She screamed for my Mam who arrived and quickly hung Robert upside while Winnie beat the shit out of his back. I panicked then, thinking he was being done over because he had stolen sweets, I ran into the dining room and put mine back. My Mam and Winnie must have known their first aid as it wasn't long before the sweet popped out onto the floor and my brother was back on his feet again. He was just over eighteen months so it must have been quite a traumatic experience for him. I said nothing and cleared off into the garden, deciding to stay out of the way for a while.

As a child I had a fascination for lions, tigers and all the animals of which I'd only seen pictures. At the top of this list of animals I hoped to see in the flesh one day were kangaroos. Our next-door neighbour George was a merchant seaman and sailed regularly between the UK and Australia. One day, when he was due to sail off again he said he would bring us back a kangaroo from Australia. The next 3 months were among the longest I recollect — we thought that George would never get home again but eventually he did.

We could not contain ourselves and Robert and I rushed next door to collect the kangaroo. 'Bad news I'm afraid', said George, 'On arrival in London the kangaroo ran away at Kings Cross station and hasn't been seen since'. This was almost the same fate as had befallen the monkey the previous year. George was a refrigeration engineer on board ship and the only consolation we had was the fact that he had brought home several large wooden cases full of Australian pears and he fed us 3 or 4 each on a daily basis. That week was when we both got infected with the chickenpox and my Mam in her concern thought that the pustules were the result of having eaten too many pears. The outcome of this was that our ration of pears was stopped, but on a more positive note, we didn't have to have a bath for around three weeks and because our heads were covered in spots we also managed to avoid the barber for a week or so.

My sister Sybil was ten years older than me and she used to get to distribute the Mars Bar. In 1951 sweets were still only obtainable under the rationing system. Rationing had been introduced during the 39-45 war to deal with food and clothing shortages, sweets remained on ration until 1953.

On a weekly basis, my Mam would send me to the local sweet shop armed with sixpence and the sweetie ration coupons to buy a Mars Bar. Overcoming temptation, I would return with the Mars Bar intact, when my sister would divide it into twelve slices. Myself and Robert got three slices each; she always got six — which included the end bits with more chocolate. At the time I thought it wasn't quite right (I was only four). If I buy a Mars Bar these days I still like to have it sliced, but now the entire bar is mine. It's just a pity they didn't have the su-per-sized bars back then like the ones you get in filling stations today, then perhaps we might all have had six slices.

Just prior to my fifth birthday was the occasion of my first journey away from home, my mother put me on board the bus in Portknockie with instructions to the conductress to put me off at Banff where my Granny would be waiting for me. My stay with Granny and Gran-dad in Banff was to last for four or five days, a long time for a wee boy. In the week before I was due to go to Banff one of my baby teeth had loosened and dropped out. My mother told me to put it below the pillow and the fairies would take away the tooth during the night and leave me a sixpence. That night the tooth went below the pillow and there was a happy chappy in the morning, a whole sixpence richer. A detailed self-examination of my teeth fol-lowed with the joyful discovery of another loose tooth, this was dislodged whilst staying at Banff, placed below my pillow and another sixpence eagerly anticipated. However, in the morning the tooth was still there and no tanner! No mention was made of this to my Granny and after returning home, the story was related to my mother. She said there was no six-pence because there weren't any fairies in Granny's garden as she didn't have any trees. Of course I believed her. Later the discovery was made that although my Granny's next door neighbours garden had no trees there was a fairy living there, but he'd joined the Merchant Navy and although he gave a lot of things away, there were never any sixpences.

Needless to say I thoroughly enjoyed my stay at Granny's, she was a good cook and baker and I got some different things to eat there. One thing I was introduced to by Granny was Birds Grape Nuts, a cereal I still enjoy for breakfast today. Granny however served them to me with warmed milk and a sprinkling of sugar. I can still smell the malty aroma. Not a lot of people eat Grape Nuts today; in fact most people I talk to have never heard of them. The taste of Grape Nuts along with Granny's oxtail soup and home made scones will be with me until I depart this earth. It was early summer when I had my stay in Banff and will never for-get being in the garden at Grannies and listening to a blackbird singing through the quiet summer air. Grandad said it was a Mavis, the old Scots name for the Song Thrush and some-times the Blackbird.

My Grandad was a boat builder and had a boat-building yard at Banff harbour. He'd come from a long line of boat-builders, originally from a family from Norway who had settled in the nearby village of Gardenstown in the 17th century. The Norwegian family name was Stefan and they ran a boatbuilding yard in Gardenstown in an area of the village still known today as Stefan's Boatyard. In later years the family name was changed to Stephen and ultimately moved the yard to The Greenbanks, an area on the left hand bank of the river Deveron in Banff. The yard was ran by the two Stephen brothers William and George. George was my great grandfather and the father to John my Grandad. The Greenbanks boatyard was later washed away after the Great War when the business relocated to Macduff. The only surviving fishing vessel built at the Greenbanks is the first class Zulu fishing boat, the 78 foot "Research" which is currently preserved indoors at the Fisheries Museum in Anstruther Fife. The Zulu features in the Bakeoff, but more of that later. I only had the one holiday with Granny in Banff as soon afterwards my Grandad sold up in Banff, retired and moved to Portknockie. Granny always said that the "Station" and the "Railway" were too close to the boatyard, both of them being pubs in Banff.

About once a year a Sikh gentleman would call round the doors in Portknockie and other villages along the coast with a large suitcase, selling or hoping to sell silk and exotic products from the east. He had a big red turban and a huge beard and fairly scared the shit out of us – at 4 years old I'd grip tightly to mother's apron whilst she spoke to him and examined his wares. We were afraid but at the same time very curious. We thought he was a bogie man and Mam used to threaten us when we misbehaved that he would come and take us away. My father used to explain to us that he was an Indian Sikh. This fact escaped my understanding at the time as he had no feathers on his head and wasn't carrying a bow & arrow; him being a "seek", as we'd heard it, just meant to us that he wasn't very well.

The Sikh gentleman was not alone in visiting the housewives of Portknockie, at the end of autumn each year we were called upon by the Ingen Johnnie, a Frenchman on a bike selling strings of onions from Brittany. On their arrival, normally in a large van full of onions and bikes we'd get a visit from the same French onion seller as we'd seen the year before and was sure to see the following year as they each had their own established 'rounds'. My Mam had been a bit of a scholar at school and had completed higher education, which included the French language. We were always amazed to hear her having a conversation with the Frenchman in his own language. She always bought two strings of onions which hung behind the kitchen door to supplement the ones we grew in the garden and would hopefully last us through the winter. That is when I learned my first bits of French; bonjour and au revoir, the Frenchman always responded with hello and cheerio. Don't quite remember when the Ingen Johnnies disappeared but I think they now sell their ingens to Lidl and Aldi.

Another caller at the door we had from time to time was a man with one leg, crutches and a tray suspended from his shoulders full of matches, needles, thread, pins and other useful bits and pieces. His leg had been amputated after a severe injury during the Great War and he was one of the ex-soldiers who returned to a land fit for heroes. Like many of his colleagues who were unable to find jobs due to disfigurement or loss of limb, the Government kindly issued them with trays of matches and other consumables and sent them out to make a living standing on street corners and calling round doors selling whatever a sympathetic public would buy. This was of course a temporary arrangement by the Government; this particular ex-soldier was still doing it over thirty years later.

Before I went off to school, I always had breakfast with Robert and Mam at nine in the morning, when Dad would come back from the bakehoose to have his porridge. One morning, in 1951 he came home at nine as usual for his breakfast, but this day he looked a bit different. His face was a funny, almost greeny/yellow colour and his eyebrows and a lot of his hair had disappeared.

The reason for his strange appearance was an explosion in the bakery. Since taking over the bakery in 1937 my father had used the existing oven, an old Scotch Oven, a bit like the modern wood burning pizza ovens, only much bigger. This oven was fired by coke which my Dad got from the gasworks in Cullen, and had to be lit at 3 o'clock each morning. Tiring of the coke oven and moving with the times he had installed a Fyna Reel Oven, heated by gas and the twelve trays inside rotated by electricity.

On this particular morning, my Dad had lit the pilot poker, stuck it in the bottom of the oven and turned on the gas supply. He then went off to get the dough out of the proving trough but returned after five minutes to check the temperature. This was when he noticed the temperature had not increased, due to the pilot poker having extinguished itself. Dad then opened the front door of the oven and threw in a lit match; due to the build of gas, there was a terrific explosion, which blew my father back about twenty feet. All this happened around 3:15 a.m., but did not stop my Dad, as he did not come home for breakfast until the usual time of 9a.m. He never tried to light the oven that way again and turned into a bit of a stickler for checking the pilot poker.

On Sundays at lunchtime, always 1 o'clock precisely, we sat down as a family to Sunday lunch, only it wasn't called lunch then, it was "yer denner". On the 10th February 1952, we were all seated round the dining table as usual, expecting to hear on the radio the voice of Billy Cotton shouting, "Wakey Wakey, it's The Billy Cotton Band Show". However, on this Sunday there was nothing but total silence emanating from the radio, the King had died on the previous Wednesday. He was only 56 and had suffered from a severe lung disorder, probably as a result of his smoking habit. Princess Elizabeth, the new Queen, was up a tree with the Duke of Edinburgh in Kenya at the time and it was nearly a year and a half before I received my enamel Coronation Mug, in those days a suitable period of mourning had to be set aside for the nation to grieve. The Coronation Mug turned out to be an extremely useful gift as it accompanied me on all the annual Sunday School picnics and to all the Christmas parties, for the tea from the urn y'understand. My Coronation Mug, though badly chipped, is still in my possession, it's in the shed full of miscellaneous screws, nuts & washers.

Before we creep on to Chapter Three here's a recipe for the all-time favourite in Scotland, Mince and Tatties with doughboys. This recipe should provide a hearty meal for four people.

Ingredients

The Mince

500g good quality minced steak, <10% fat

2 medium and 1 large carrot

1 slice of swede about 1/4" thick

1 large onion

1/2 to 3/4 pint beef stock + a drop of gravy browning if you prefer a darker gravy

The Potatoes

500g of Kerr's Pink, Desiree or Rooster potatoes

The Doughboys

4 large tablespoons SR flour

1 level tsp baking powder

2 tablespoons vegetable suet

Salt & pepper

A little cold water to bind

METHOD

The Mince

First look out a suitable saucepan and prepare the vegetables. Chop the onion finely and dice the two medium carrots, about 5mm square is fine, do the swede the same size. Prepare the large carrot and split in half lengthways then cut into two-inch pieces - this gives you another vegetable to serve with the dish.

Melt some lard or oil in your saucepan and brown the onion with a teaspoon of sugar. Add the minced steak a little at a time and brown. Finally add your prepared vegetables, salt and pepper and the stock and simmer for around 45 minutes to one hour. You'll know when it has been cooked enough when the carrot and swede are soft and a fork will pass easily through the larger pieces of carrot.

Potatoes

Peel the potatoes and cut into even sized pieces, cover with water and a teaspoon of salt.

The Doughboys

Mix the flour, baking powder, salt & pepper and suet with the water to make a soft dough. Using a little flour to prevent sticking, divide into four pieces and roll into balls.

With the mince cooked and returned to simmer, place the four doughboys on top of the mince, remembering to replace the saucepan lid. At the same time put the potatoes on to boil. When the potatoes are boiled, strain and mash with a small knob of butter a little milk and some freshly ground black pepper. When properly mashed, beat well with a wooden spoon - this adds a creaminess to the potatoes, which you only get with the wooden spoon treatment. I always use my favourite wooden spoon, which I also used at the Bakeoff; it's my "Runcible Spoon" - thanks to Edward Lear. By this time, you should find that the doughboys have risen to be light and fluffy.

Serve the mince, doughboys and mashed potatoes with your favourite vegetable(s).

I always find that cabbage, in particular Savoy Cabbage, finely shredded, and cooked with caraway seed and black pepper to be a particularly enjoyable accompaniment.

A note on using swede........

Although the above dish can be prepared without adding vegetables, you will find that the addition of swede or 'neeps' to Scottish bred beef gives your gravy a superb flavour. This may have something to do with the fact that the best-reared beef cattle in Scotland have a winter diet supplemented by 'neeps'.

CHAPTER THREE
Applying for The Bakeoff

It was the 14th of January 2014 and, finding myself at a loose end, I was browsing the web when I came across the application form for potential contestants for the Great British Bakeoff Series Five. The deadline for applications was the 17th of January 2014, so I completed the application online and submitted it, not expecting to hear anything further. You can imagine my surprise when next day I received a telephone call from a researcher at Love Productions who carried out a short telephone interview. The researcher said that if my application was going any further I might receive another telephone call. The following day I had another call and a second interview asking about my baking experience and a few technical questions regarding baking. Again I was told that if there was no further contact it would mean that's as far as the application was going and, of course, they stressed once more that you've done very well to get this far. They have this knack at Love Productions of always displaying an extremely positive attitude and invariably leave you feeling good about yourself. I can recall thinking that I would not be telling anyone I had been talking to Love Productions; they may well assume I was making a porn film!

At this point I was requested to provide references from responsible individuals, employers etc. I didn't really know any responsible people but I quickly contacted a lifelong friend, Mrs Carol Watt who with husband Jimmy, runs the West End Guest House in Elgin and she readily agreed to supply the necessary testimonial. My second referee was Sonia Ingleton who had been my manager for a while at GlaxoSmithkline in London, and Sonia too was happy to provide feedback for Love Productions.

The references must have done the trick as within a few days, Love had invited me to attend an audition in Manchester and to bring one sweet and one savoury item of baking with me. Well, Manchester is a long way from Buckie but as we had never been there before Iris and I decided to go. We booked a train journey from Keith to Manchester and got up very early on the 20th January to do a spot of baking before setting off for Keith to board the train for Aberdeen and

Manchester. Love had already informed me that they would not pay expenses for the journey, but we were treating this as a small holiday so were not too bothered about the expense. Having a railcard helped, and made the travel cost a wee bit cheaper.

Out of bed at five am, I made a jalousie aux pommes, which is an apple pie with puff pastry in the shape of a French window shutter plus a dozen cheese, sun dried tomato and pesto rolls, a bit like savoury Chelsea buns. I had prepared everything the previous evening including making the puff pastry and the home made pesto, a couple of items that could have been a bit time consuming. The baking went well and after getting a lift to the railway station at Keith from my brother Robert, we were on board the Manchester bound train at Aberdeen before lunchtime. Robert was quite pleased with himself as he was looking after Lucy our Mini Schnauzer for a few days; Lucy was chuffed as well as she really likes her Uncle Robert – he lets her sleep at the end of his bed.

The journey south went very smoothly and we soon arrived safely at The Victoria Warehouse Project Hotel in Manchester, in the neighbourhood of Old Trafford. This was a very economically priced hotel, and was in fact an old warehouse recently converted; I had found it on the Internet whilst looking for a Travelodge. There were no frills like a fountain or grand piano in the foyer but the rooms were perfect; we had a great night's sleep followed by an excellent breakfast, all for the princely sum of £79 for two nights for two people. The sauce for the pudding was finding out how friendly the people of Manchester were; from the young lad on reception at the Warehouse Hotel to the waitress at The Hard Rock and all the people in between we had spoken to regarding directions etc., they were all as we say at home, "brand new". It is also interesting to note that the taxi drivers we met were very well dressed in suit, shirt and tie. A welcome change from the normal casual dress and egg-stained tee shirt! On one occasion, many years ago I had to travel to the Railway Station at Dyce from Aberdeen Heliport. On the way, the taxi driver finished off a bag of crisps; after disposing of the empty bag through his open window, he then proceeded to remove his upper set of dentures and lick the plate. He remarked on the joy of having false teeth, adding; "You can always get a second helping". That of course was after he had had a moan about the Dyce Railway Station being recently reopened, saying that if it wasn't open he would've had a fare into Aberdeen, at my expense of course. Had I been in the habit of giving tips, he definitely would not have received one that day. Our taxi to take me to the audition arrived on time, our first stop at the Marks and Spencer store to drop off Iris, which was the main reason of course for us travelling to Manchester!

At the audition, about ten of us had our photographs taken with our bakes, at which stage, after observing what the others had baked and brought, I decided this could well be the end of the road for me. The standard of the bakes people had brought along was awe-inspiring, in particular the line-up of gateaux and elaborately decorated cakes. My own stuff looked very plain and simple in comparison but I guess that is just my style. An interview by two home economists then followed and Louise, a runner for Love Productions, said that if they liked my bakes and me I would then have a screen test. Next, they gave me a cup of coffee and asked me to wait. Surprise, surprise, they gave me a 30 minute interview on camera with Anna Driver, one of the senior producers with Love Productions. They later thanked me for my time spent in coming to the interview; I left the bakes behind and went to find Mrs.C at the shopping centre. We had a pulled pork sandwich in the M&S restaurant – another first for me, I enjoyed it so much I have started to pull my pork at home, if we have a roast on a Sunday. After lunch we completed the shopping and decided to go to the movies. American Hustle had just been released so that's the one we chose, later visiting The Hard Rock Cafe for what was probably the best pint of Stella Artois I've had in a long time. It was so good I had another one prior to dining on a superb sirloin steak whilst Iris had a hamburger and salad (the budget would not run to two steaks). We later returned to the Warehouse for a nightcap and retired to bed, sleeping very well after a fantastic day and an extremely positive experience.

The following day we travelled north by train and life carried on at home as normal, but only for a short while as very soon I was contacted again by Love who asked me to attend a further audition, this time in London. This did not present us with any problems, as it would be nice to travel south again and be able to see the girls, who live in Stoke Newington. Love sent me two recipes, one for scones and one for a loaf of bread, both standard recipes that I had to bake and bring to London. I took the decision to drive to London as this would save time and allow me to complete the necessary baking before leaving. We arose around four in the morning; I baked the scones and the bread and set off for the six hundred and twenty-five mile journey. As I did not intend to drive into London due to parking problems etc., I had booked the Travelodge at Hatfield for a night; this enabled us to drive from Hatfield in the morning to Welwyn Garden City where we would leave the car in the multi-storey car park within the Howard Centre next to the railway station. From Welwyn it is a short journey to Kings Cross and then a bus ride to the location of the audition.

The journey south was uneventful, just a quick stop at the House of Bruar with another at Tebay on the M6 for fuel and food, arriving at Hatfield around ten pm. In the morning, we set off for London and after parking the car in the Howard Centre in Welwyn Garden City, boarded the train for Kings Cross. Iris then headed for the V&A Museum to meet Louise during her lunch hour and I headed for the audition. I caught the 205 bus to Old Street and had a leisurely stroll to the audition location at Hackney College, about twenty minutes away. I met Jamie McIntosh again, who had taken our photographs at Manchester. Also present were two other bakers who would eventually win through, one was Diana whom I had met previously at the Manchester audition and the other was Jordan. I met the other eleven bakers who were present for the audition and was introduced to Murray Grindon, who was later to play a crucial role in the Bakeoff itself. A home economist and a food producer interviewed us before we were let loose in a large kitchen with twelve ovens and workstations. In this kitchen area, there were four camera crews, their task was to film and interview us as we baked. After donning our aprons we were given the obligatory health and safety talk, handed a recipe, then allocated a workstation and told to "bake". We had been told that there would be a "technical challenge" and of course, our minds had been working overtime trying to guess what we might have to bake. All kinds of strange and complicated scenarios went through our heads, so you can imagine the collective sigh of relief when our "challenge" was revealed, we had to bake a carrot cake, and I think just over an hour was allowed for the bake. At the end of this exercise, we had all turned out almost identical cakes, apart from Diana who had taken a bit more time on the finishing and presentation. We then had further interviews and told once more that we would be contacted if we were chosen to progress to the next stage.

By this time, it was late afternoon so I set off for Stoke Newington and met up with Iris and the girls. They were becoming excited about the prospects of me being part of The Bakeoff as they have been all along of course, now they are convinced I will be on it. A friend of Corinne's who works in the "business" was convinced that with me being Scottish and called Norman I would be guaranteed a place. We ended the day with a trip to YumYums, reputedly the biggest Thai restaurant in Europe, certainly the biggest one I have seen. Despite its size, it has a lovely at-mosphere and a well-appointed cocktail bar and waiting area. A few drinks and a delightful meal helped me say goodbye to another £120, which is a reasonable price I suppose for dinner for four in London. In truth London prices are not much more than the North-east of Scotland especially Aberdeen. However, don't panic, it's not really Aberdonians spending the money as there has been a huge influx of many nationalities due to the growth of the oil industry in and around Aberdeen.

Stoke Newington is a nice area to live in and well provided for in the transport stakes, with Un-derground, Overground and lots of buses. The girls do enjoy living there. It is also unique in that there are no "chain" restaurants but instead a delightful range of small independent coffee shops, tea rooms, restaurants, pubs and bakeries, quite refreshing really. The High Street news-agent is also a unique establishment as he advertises his business as "Porn Free". There is an old warehouse in Stoke Newington where they filmed the first episodes of Dragons Den. The large graveyard, Abney Park, in the town centre is the last resting place of none other than the founder of the Salvation Army, General William Booth. It is also home to a branch of World Foods, the others in London being in Kensington High Street, Camden and Piccadilly, well worth a visit if you are visiting London, in particular the one in Kensington, which is huge. Corinne and Louise rent a large property in Stokey and share it with one other so that is where we spent the night after our visit to YumYums.

The following morning we made our way to Kings Cross where we boarded the fast train to Welwyn Garden City and within thirty minutes we were setting off in the car, having paid the bargain sum of eight pounds for the parking. We headed northwest and picked up the M6 for the journey north and appreciated the low traffic volume, it was Sunday of course so we had a leisurely drive up the M6, before deciding to stop for the night in Carlisle. We parked outside the Travelodge in Carlisle City Centre and logged on to their website using their WiFi signal. This way, if you book the room online you save yourself a fiver. This we did and got ourselves a room for the night. We then set out to have a quiet drink and a meal. We found a Weatherspoon's pub and had one of their buy one get one free meals, surprisingly very good with a drink included, under ten pounds for the two of us. You could not make it for that! After a quick stop at the House of Bruar on the A9, where incidentally the two cups of coffee and shared sandwich cost more than our meal and drink the previous evening in Carlisle, we carried on to Aviemore and then home. We arrived home early on Sunday evening and first of all called at Robert's to collect Lucy, who was swinging from the chandeliers she was so overjoyed to see us.

All went very quiet on the Bakeoff front with no further communication from Love until quite late on Friday 21st February. That was when I received a telephone call from Anna to inform me that I was now on the list of the final fourteen candidates for the GBBO 2014; the final twelve eventually being selected from this fourteen, again it was stressed how well I had done to get this far. With me selected as one of the final fourteen, Love Productions now had to prepare a back-story for me. The sixth of March was to be the day that Anna would arrive complete with a camera crew. This gave Iris nearly fourteen days to clean the house, not enough time she said, and spent the next fortnight flying around like a tornado. You would have thought the Queen was coming, although she did stop short of redecorating the place. Lucy and myself were kind of wishing we had gone away for a week or so.

Finally, it was Friday 6th of March and Anna arrived, accompanied by Tim the cameraman and Louise the runner. They started work at nine a.m., and we thought they would be gone by lunchtime. Wrong. They filmed me in the kitchen making bread and éclairs, in the caravan making sausage rolls and in the shed doing pottery.

We then went to Portknockie and they filmed Lucy and me walking near the Bow Fiddle Rock. Then it was back to the house to film me making beer. They finally departed for Aberdeen and their flight to London around five p.m. We were exhausted and still did not know if I was going to be in the final twelve or not, that revelation was still to come. On Friday the 13th March, I had a further phone call quite late on, congratulating me on making it through to the final twelve for the GBBO 2014. This was when the hard work began.

Before we move on to Chapter Four and more about my early life, I thought this would be an opportune moment to let you have my recipe for the jalousie aux pommes....................

Jalousie aux Pommes

Ingredients

Puff Pastry

225g Plain flour

175g butter

100ml cold water (approx.)

Filling

400g Bramley cooking apples

200g Dessert apples

Juice of one lemon

100g caster sugar

Method

Cut butter into small cubes around 5cm square and divide this into 4 equal portions. In a large bowl, rub one portion of butter into the flour and add one pinch of salt. Add cold water to make a soft dough.

Roll out dough to a rectangular strip and dot two thirds of the dough with another portion of butter. Fold over the one third of the dough with no butter over the centre part of the strip, and then fold the remaining piece over this. Wrap in cling film or a polythene bag and chill for thirty minutes. Repeat this process twice more and chill the pastry for an hour before using.

If you are in a hurry, you could always use shop-bought puff pastry.

Peel, core and slice the dessert apples, add to a saucepan with one teaspoon mixed spice and three cloves. Cook until consistency resembles an apple puree and remove the cloves. Set aside to cool.

Peel, core and slice the Bramley apples; place in a bowl and cover with the juice of the lemon and then sprinkle over the caster sugar.

Once the apples are cool divide the pastry into two equal portions and roll out each piece to a rectangle around 20cm x 15cm. Fold over one piece lengthwise and make cuts with a sharp knife through three quarters of the fold and around 5cm apart. Place the apple puree on the other piece of pastry and place the Bramley apple slices on top. Brush the edges with milk or beaten egg and cover with the slatted piece of pastry. Seal all round the edges, brush with a little milk, sprinkle with caster sugar and bake at 200 degrees centigrade for thirty to thirty-five minutes or until nicely browned.

Serve hot or cold with ice cream, cream or custard. This dessert should serve six people.

CHAPTER FOUR

Off to School

Among my early memories of school is the first day in Primary One; the teacher was a Miss Crowsfeet. They were all 'misses' in those days with one or two exceptions. They were mostly quite elderly (or so it appeared to us) and most of them came with a fearsome reputation. I remember getting a small blackboard and a piece of white chalk on the first day. Most of the mothers stayed behind for an hour or so to wipe away the tears. Some of my classmates had brought a biscuit or 'piece' with them to eat during the mid-morning break. Those who had no 'piece' were able to buy, for the sum of one halfpenny, a Rich tea biscuit that the teacher sold from a tin under her desk. We also got a third of a pint of milk; remember these were pre-Thatcher days.

Miss Crowsfeet was very nice to us all on the first day – many of the mothers were still present of course. Later on in the week, she showed her true colours when Jackie Watson wanted to go to the toilet. She would not let him go so he just stood there and the inevitable happened - he wet himself. The kind of underpants we wore back then facilitated the smooth passage of anything down the leg, not like the modern ones, which offer a degree of containment. I will never forget the sight of him as he stood there with yellow stuff running down his leg and the teacher shouting at him. Jackie then ran home and never came back that week.

Week two at school was when I went off milk for life. There was either condensation on my third of a pint bottle or the milk was leaking. Anyway, the bottle slipped from my little hand, bounced off the desk and spilt all over the lassie who sat next to me. I cannot remember her name, but after that accident, my milk was stopped for a week. I responded by never drinking milk again, a trait which has lasted to this day. I do not think I ever liked the stuff before that anyway, I used to say milk is for babies.

From the first day in Primary One, every morning at nine o'clock we had an assembly of the entire school in the main hall. Mr Moyes the Dominie or Headmaster entered from behind the assembled pupils and teachers, bearing a bible in his hand along with some notes for the day's work and addressed the congregation. He then started the proceedings with a singing version of the Lord's Prayer. None of us really managed to grasp what the phrase "forgive us our trespasses as we forgive those who trespass against us" meant and could not pronounce it properly until we were a bit older. To this day I still do not have a clue what that really meant, one of the older boys told us later that it was to do with picking your nose, but we were never sure about that. A hymn, usually All Things Bright and Beautiful or When He Cometh and occasionally a rousing one like Onward Christian Soldiers or Thine Be the Glory then followed the chanting of the Lord's Prayer. Needless to say, as we matured in school, many of the boys had their own words for some of the hymns; I'll not print those lest we cause offence. After a short prayer and shouting of "amen", (all 200 or so of us) went to our various classrooms to commence another joyous day of enforced education. If a pupil didn't appear for school, the janitor (Mr Geddes) would be despatched to their home to find out why - and they had to be ill. No one was allowed to miss a minute of this fine programme of learning

In the 1950's Mr Moyes's position as Headmaster of the school carried a high degree of status and he was probably regarded in the same light as the doctor, solicitor or minister of the kirk. Indeed, Mr Moyes would deputise for the minister at the local Church of Scotland when required. Today, if one heads to the east end of Portknockie, taking the coastal path past the Bow Fiddle Rock then following the path and steps down past the Whales Moo, not far from the start of Portknockie's sandy beach and golf course, you will come across the Preachers Cave. This cave has been used over the centuries as a home for travelling folks, an illegal gambling den and as a temporary place of worship. In the 18th century when the Church of Scotland and the Free Church had a dispute, the Free Church migrated their services to the Preachers Cave. On Sunday 26th July 1936, a Christian service took place in this cave. It was reported at the time that a congregation of 500 attended to hear Mr Moyes conduct the service and give the address. Although only a limited number could be accommodated in the cave itself the crowd outside could hear the service adequately due to the loudspeakers which had been set up by Harry Watson, Banff. G.A.Scrimgeour (he could be straight out of Dickens), Portknockie Town Clerk, read the lesson, with the singing of songs of praise being led by Jocky Skelly, coal merchant. It must have been incredibly arousing to listen to 500 people standing outdoors and emptying their lungs to How Great Thou Art, regardless of religious persuasion, or even Will Your Anchor Hold to the sound of breaking surf on the nearby beach.

A collection of £20 was taken on that memorable day and shared between Chalmers Hospital, Banff and Aberdeen Hospital. Mr MacIntosh, Wembley, Forgue lent a marquee tent for the occasion; (MacIntosh O'Forgue was an infamous scrap dealer & horse trader and friend of my father). The marquee tent was set up near the bowling green where the Town Clerk, Mr Scrimgeour, entertained a number of guests. It was also reported at the time that some elders of the church and a few local dignitaries strongly disapproved of worshipping the Lord in such a frivolous fashion and this on the Lords Day. Today it would be wonderful to see such an event again but it would probably be disallowed owing to the health and safety and other concerns that abound in the age we live in...pity.

Slates and slate pencils, that's what sticks out most in my mind about Primary One at Portknockie. As to learning the alphabet, my time in Primary Two was halfway over before I successfully managed to recite the alphabet from start to finish, definitely a slow learner. One of my recollections is of being given a box of coloured squares, two of each colour and told to match them up. My tiny mind didn't have a clue what this meant and did what I thought was 'matching' by pairing black with white (an obvious one), then red with green followed by brown and yellow, this left me with blue and pink, again fairly obvious. Miss Crowsfeet just shook her head at my effort but made no attempt to tell me what was actually required. That was when she decided to sit me at the front of the class. That is the way it was in the fifties, the greater your presumed intelligence the farther toward the back of the class you would be sitting. Some years at school had passed before I found out that matching meant getting hold of two things the same colour, size, shape etc. Just a wee bit slow on the uptake you would say, not quite the sharpest knife in the drawer. I was almost fifteen years old before finding myself located far enough from the front for it not to matter. By that time of course I considered that having a view of Anne Forsyth's legs to have a higher priority than my position in the class seating.

As mentioned earlier I had given up drinking milk soon after starting in Primary One and it wasn't very long afterwards that I stopped eating eggs. My father kept chickens or hens as we called them, he had around two hundred of them and used most of the eggs in the bakery. One day while helping my mother to collect the eggs, I picked up an egg that a hen had been sitting on, accidentally dropped it and revealed inside a half formed chicken. Eating eggs thereafter was something I avoided and was well into my teens before going near one again. Even now there's no way I could eat a soft-boiled egg, I cannot even bear to watch anyone else do so either. If I see someone dipping "soldiers" into a soft egg, I just want to vomit. Besides the hens, my Dad also kept pigs, ducks and turkeys. He normally had around thirty turkeys bred each year for Christmas and New Year dinners. He would sell the turkeys locally and because they were usually very big, in excess of 15 lbs and no one had an oven big enough to accommodate them; he always cooked them on Christmas and New Year's Day in the oven in the bakery. One New Year's Day lunch we had one, which supposedly weighted a massive thirty-two pounds; it served over a dozen for the meal that day and we were still having soup with a turkey bone derived stock in the middle of January.

Days in the classroom in Primary One seemed to last forever, we always thought that half-past three would never come round but eventually the days wore on and it wasn't long before we returned to school after the Easter holidays and were marched off into the Primary Two classroom.

It could have been said that Miss Crowsfeet was no angel but once we had experienced a day under the tutelage of Miss Scrotal we started to realise that perhaps our first teacher had indeed descended from Heaven. Miss Scrotal, we believed, was on first name terms with 'Auld

Nick' himself and had attended the Devils College for teachers. She could inflict pain without leaving much of a mark and was an expert at hitting you over the knuckles with the edge of her ruler. Any movement other than that necessary to read or write was expressly forbidden. To ensure we did not move whilst not reading or writing we had to sit on our hands. I cannot recall one happy day in her class, except perhaps the last one.

Being pupils of Miss Scrotal gave us all quite a shock but one day we got an inkling that she may indeed have possessed a heart. We had a new pupil arrive, Jimmy Gordon. Jimmy was from a family of travelling people and arrived at school in November with no boots or shoes on his feet. Miss Scrotal then asked the class if anyone could bring along a pair of boots for Jimmy. I think it was Donald Morrison who made a positive response and the following day Jimmy had boots on his feet. This brought what we thought may have been a smile to Miss Scrotal's face; on the other hand perhaps it was just wind.

Looking back at my time under Miss Scrotal I find it hard to recall any joyous moments. It was 1953, the year of the coronation of Queen Elizabeth when Winston Churchill was our Prime Minister. At six years of age, my belief was still that Winston Churchill was a friend of my Grandad and my father made bread for the Queen. Who else would she buy bread from I had thought. My Father was always telling people how good his bread was so what else was a child to think. The World was a small place inside a small mind in 1953. However, I did manage to tell Miss Scrotal one day that the Queen got her bread from my Dad, she said, and I can honestly remember this; she said, "Stupid boy". Capt. Mainwaring eat yer socks.

Early in 1953, we experienced what was probably the storm of the century. On the 31st January, the east coast of the UK experienced high tides and very strong winds. Sheds disappeared from gardens, boats were wrecked at their moorings, whole acres of forest were devastated and hundreds of lives lost.

My father had wooden stables and a garage near where he kept the hens and pigs. During the storm, the stables were completely wrecked. The memory is still alive of going to see the damage with Mam, holding tightly on to her hand lest I be blown away, and I can recall a large plank of wood suddenly flying through the air above our heads. When this was followed by three hens, my mother decided to return to the safety of the house. The stable being wrecked was a great disappointment to me; when it was standing it had a ladder inside leading to a loft and in the loft were several boxes of old junk. There were bits of old clocks, an old gramophone and all kinds of bits and pieces, which I would spend hours sorting through. My best discovery in the old loft was a box of old bullets or as soldiers refer to them "rounds", these were mainly .303 rounds. Incidentally, they were called rounds because during the days of muskets firing musket balls, soldiers of the time would prefer a "round" ball as opposed to a misshapen or elongated one. If you used pliers, it was possible to separate the bullet from the detonator cartridge, thereby giving access to the cordite inside. When lit with a match the cordite made quite a spectacular flash. Unfortunately, the paraphernalia of the loft disappeared after the gale never to be seen again. The wrecked buildings were replaced later in the year with a huge garage capable of holding four vehicles but unfortunately, there was no loft. The reconstruction work was carried out by none other than Jock Henderson the railway signalman and husband of Mrs H who had delivered me and brother Robert. The Henderson's were indeed a useful family to know.

Miss Scrotal was at last left behind when we graduated to Primary Three under the care of a very kind lady, Miss Watson. Miss Watson was the opposite of anything we had heard or experienced about teachers. She was a warm and generous soul who never once to my knowledge raised her voice nor indulged in any form of corporal punishment. She taught with kindness and the class responded well. Prior to joining her class, I had difficulty reading aloud, due mainly to being nervous rather than a having a reading problem. It was just a pity that due to an injury I received one Sunday, I missed a few weeks of her teaching. My mother always said it was the Lord taking His revenge on me for what I'd done.

At 2 o'clock every Sunday afternoon, my Mother would give me two pennies and send me off to learn more about God and Jesus under the guidance of Miss Donaldson at the Church of Scotland Sunday School. Sunday the 14th of June 1954 was no exception, dressed in my little brown suit I was despatched to Sunday School. I liked the brown suit, it was a welcome change from the Jock Frock my mother had made for me at four years of age. My first outing to Sunday School at four was a nightmare as I'd turned up the only boy dressed in a kilt and there was a lot of ribbing regarding my appearance. Back to the 14th of June, I'd met my best pal Kenneth on the way to Sunday School, only we didn't call him Kenneth then. As Kenneth was a wee bit overweight for his age and we being non politically correct in those days he was always known as Fatty. I always used to think he looked a bit like Fat Boab from the cartoon page, Oor Wullie in the Sunday Post.

On our way to Sunday School our normal path led us past the local newsagents shop - Charlie Tosh's. This Sunday became an exception, we didn't go past. You see Charlie had a chewing gum vending machine outside his shop and in those days you got two packets of gum for 1p if the arrow on the dispensing handle was pointing forward. Our luck was in that day or so we thought; the arrow was pointing forward. Fatty's' mother had been a tad more generous that Sunday and he'd been given three pennies, one of which went in the machine. Fatty now had two packets of gum. I then put in a penny followed by my second penny. This left the arrow on the handle then pointing upward. It didn't take Fatty long to deduce that another two pennies would net three packets of gum. This left us with seven packets of chewing gum but unfortunately nothing to put on the collection plate whilst we sang; "Hear the pennies dropping, Count them as they fall, Every one for Jesus, He shall have them all". This Sunday however Jesus wasn't going to get them all, as Charlie Tosh now had ours and Jesus certainly had no chance of getting the gum; so we abandoned all hope of redemption as we walked past the Church door, down the Bakers Brae and chewed our way to the harbour.

The tide was out when we reached the harbour so we played on the sand and checked out the rock pools, round about the area where the paddling pool now sits. Tiring of that we decided to walk along the top of the harbour breakwater toward the lighthouse. We scrambled up the Tarry Rock and started to walk toward the other end. Unfortunately, I tripped, slipped or stumbled; not sure which and fell to my right, about a ten-foot drop on to the main quay. The lucky part of this was that I had fallen to my right, had it been to my left, then I think I would have drowned after a twenty-foot or so fall. As it was, I landed on the quay with my right elbow hitting the quayside first. We walked back and played around on the sand for a while until I started to feel a lot of pain from my elbow. I took off my jacket and Fatty decided that as it was not hanging off, it wasn't broken. I eventually made my way home and collapsed in the armchair next to the Rayburn in the kitchen.

My mother and father returned from their afternoon stroll around 4pm; my mother took a look at me, realised something was wrong and said to my father, "Davie, fit's adee wi' this bairn he's a face lik' the back o' a plate."* I had indeed turned white and was unable to get out of the chair and howled like a banshee when my father took hold of my right arm. I was immediately put to bed and Dr. Thomson summoned. Dr Thomson was our family GP and knew my father from way back as my dad as a teenager had driven Dr.Thomsons father, who was also a doctor, in his pony and trap and later his motor car. This was somewhere in Aberdeenshire, it could have been Alford but I am not exactly sure on that. Dr.Thomson was not a happy bunny having had his Sunday afternoon disrupted and non-too happy with me either as I didn't tell him exactly what had happened, I daren't have told him as I knew I shouldn't have been anywhere near the harbour on a Sunday. Eventually I was despatched in the back of my father's car to Dr.Gray's hospital in Elgin.

*(David, what's wrong with this child, his face is awfully white)

At Dr.Gray's an interrogation took place led by a man in a white coat who finally deduced that I'd fallen off a high wall but had only hurt my arm; in fact, it was broken. There was no apparent evidence of any other injury to my body. I do not recall much more about what happened that Sunday but will never forget being anaesthetised with chloroform. They put a thing like a large tea strainer over my nose and mouth and poured some stuff from a bottle over it, to this day the smell recurs from time to time. The last image in my mind when they put me to sleep was of 3 or 4 people standing round me, they turned into eight or more then multiplied until there were hundreds of Red Indians dancing round me. The following morning found me with my right arm bent at ninety degrees inside a white plaster cast, in a bed at the end of a ward full of what appeared to be a bunch of old men but most of them, I discovered later, were around middle age or younger. A nurse then appeared and took the clipboard from the end of my bed. She stuck a thermometer under my arm and asked me if my bowels had moved; my reply was that it wasn't me, I never touched them.

The hospital had allocated me a bed in the adult male ward, as the children's ward was full at the time of my admission. This was a good thing for me as I received lots of attention that I would not otherwise have been given in the children's ward. On the Tuesday morning, I received a copy of the Dandy from one of the men in the ward. This made me feel at home as Tuesday was the day we normally got it delivered in Portknockie. My fingers were then crossed for Thursday as that was the day the Beano was issued. I always considered that the Beano was a superior comic to the Dandy, a case of Biffo The Bear v. Korky The Kat.

On the Monday afternoon my Mam paid me a visit bringing some rice biscuits and an extended lecture on the perils of evading Sunday School. This talking-to had a lasting effect and I do not think I missed a Day at Sunday School until I was fifteen. The visit was over all too quickly and when she left I crawled under the blanket and cried my heart out. I'd thought that I might have been going home with my mother but didn't see her again until the Wednesday, only two days but which seemed at the time an eternity. Looking back, my daily life in the hospital seemed to be filled with a lot of new and strange words being used by the nursing staff. There was a male nurse in the ward who wore very thick crepe soled shoes, which made a loud squeaking noise with every step he took. I had also heard him refer to the "Staff Nurse" and me being me, I was then on the lookout for a nurse with a staff, I thought she was either lame or had some connection with God and the Sunday School. This stemmed from us having sung the 23rd Psalm, The

Lord's My Shepherd at school and Sunday school, "for Thou art with me, thy rod and staff me comfort still".

Ending up in hospital wasn't nearly as bad an experience as I had feared prior to breaking my arm. As a very young child you hear about other kids having their tonsils removed. Despite the fact that you are fed a diet of ice cream and jelly for days afterwards, it was still not something you would want to queue up for. My father told me he had said goodbye to his own tonsils on his Aunt's kitchen table in Orchard Street, Aberdeen, before the Great War. Must have been hell then. As you grow up you learn about all the things that can go wrong with your health at different ages. At around eight or nine the big fear moved from the tonsils to having to have your appendix removed. This easily out-classed anything else as a something to be dreaded, as they ripped you open for that. Later on of course we had to contend with polio and leukaemia as major threats to our existence. Eventually, after joining the Merchant Navy most of my fears centred round STD's. Diseases like gonorrhoea, syphilis and green monkey disease became the new threats to good health. As ageing adults we start to worry about hypertension, heart at-tacks and hip replacements. Seems as if there's always a something waiting in the wings for us. Once you start to collect your pension you stop worrying about the clap as the focus is then on cancer and alchoheimers disease, but as my brother-in-law Stanley Bowie used to say "What's cancer if you've got your health!"

Although homesick for periods of time in the hospital, the passing of the days was assisted by me becoming more mobile and walking around the ward and also by being given lots of comics; Biffo The Bear, Lord Snooty and his pals to say nothing of Little Plum Your Redskin Chum helped enormously to shorten the days. Eventually it was Monday 22nd June and my Mam arrived complete with a birthday cake and a small model racing car. It was a Maserati in British Racing Green with the number 7 on the side, the favoured number at the time of Stirling Moss. It was a wind-up model and I had endless hours of fun on the ward floor with this new toy. There was a downside to having my birthday in the hospital; they brought all the children (at least all those who could walk) into the ward. They then made a circle round my bed and sang Happy

Birthday, I found the whole process deeply embarrassing and immediately dived below the bed covers. It was early July before I was eventually collected by my Mam and taken home, I do not recall the exact date but the sun was shining and I was dressed in my Sloppy Joe (a tee-shirt), my khaki shorts and sandals - the ones with very hard stiff soles that felt like bits of wood on your feet. The arm was still bent and in plaster with the weight being borne by a sling round my neck. The tragedy of the day, however, was the fact that I had left my model racing car behind in the hospital and I never saw it again.

Scotch Broth always made a regular appearance on the menu at Summerton; quite often, a dead hen was boiled up in the pot and gave added flavour to the broth. I have included a recipe, which closely resembles what my mother made, I know because I watched her do it plenty of times. So here it is – minus the dead hen, of course, but with a nice piece of silverside.

Ingredients

500g Silverside salmon cut

1 swede

4 large carrots

1 leek

1 piece of kale leaf

1 onion

150g proprietary broth mix

salt and pepper

2 litres water

1 vegetable stock cube

Method

Prepare the vegetables.

Peel the carrots.

Chop one carrot into small dice.

Grate one carrot.

Cut the other two carrots in half.

Cut the swede in half and use just the one half.

Peel the swede and divide in three.

Chop one third of the swede into fine dice and leave the other two pieces whole.

Chop the leek and the kale finely.

Place the meat in a large saucepan or soup pot with two litres of water, salt & pepper and bring to the boil, then simmer for forty minutes before adding the vegetable stock cube and the 150g of broth mix cereals.

Simmer for a further 20 minutes then add all the carrot, swede and leek.

Return to simmer for a further 90 minutes and then add the kale.

Simmer for another 30 minutes and at the same time peel, boil and mash 500g of potatoes; Maris Piper, Kerr's Pink or Roosters.

Remove the chunks of swede and carrot along with the beef to a casserole dish and keep warm. Serve the broth.

Serve the beef and vegetables with the mashed potato; usually this is served in the same plate as you ate the soup from. Remember also to lick your soup spoon clean as it will be required for the pudding.

Quite often, my Mother would also make a "mealie dumpling", boiled in a muslin cloth in the soup pot. This was a mixture of oatmeal, suet, onion, seasoning, size and sage, similar to haggis without the bits of offal.

This is a meal guaranteed to *"bring you back from the jaws of death"* and will certainly prepare you well for recipe creation and for the first week of The Great British Bakeoff.

CHAPTER FIVE

The Recipes

Setting out to write a book would, I had assumed, be quite a demanding task; designing a plot and creating many different characters is a challenge for even the most talented of writers. Therefore, although I had thought it would be an onerous task to create my autobiography, it has so far been relatively easy as I already have the plot and I know all the characters personally. I say easy but what I really mean is that putting my life on paper has been quite straightforward in comparison to the next task set by the GBBO Team. After we had officially been told of our success in qualifying to take part in the Bakeoff 2015, we were then introduced to Chloe. Chloe Avery that is and on the 3rd of March she sent us the first of the many recipe requests we would receive every two weeks. We would then have to create the recipe, complete test bakes, tweak the recipe, bake it again and when satisfied, submit it to Chloe. She would then call us the following week to discuss the recipe and make any suggestions or adjustments; "Would that be large eggs?", "Is that salted or unsalted butter?", "What equipment will you be bringing with you?" and so on. I would say by the time I was submitting recipes for Programmes 7 & 8, I was just about getting the hang of it.

The first recipe requests were for Programmes One and Two. The Week One recipes required were in the Cakes category and we were asked to submit for approval our recipes for our Signature Swiss Roll and the Showstopper Display of Miniature British Cakes. The Week Two recipe requests were for our Signature Savoury Biscuits and The Showstopper was for a 3-D Biscuit Display. Quite straightforward, you would think and as we had been given a deadline of 17th March, I thought the same, not a problem. However St. Patrick's day seemed to arrive in double quick time; fortunately I had decided which recipes I'd use and even managed to test them a couple of times. It was further reinforced that we should not copy recipes direct from a book nor indeed cut and paste from the Internet.

To start with, I composed a recipe and baked a plain and simple Swiss Roll, filled with cream and homemade raspberry jam. The taste was superb and it looked good as well, might even have won a prize at the SWRI monthly meeting. I tentatively submitted this recipe to Chloe and was told that if I wanted to do well in the Bakeoff I would need to create something a touch more demanding. I asked Chloe what she would like me to do and I suggested quite out of the blue a Black Forest Swiss Roll. Chloe thought that was a great idea so I then set about trying to imagine what one of these would look like and began experimenting with chocolate type Swiss Rolls. Personally, the first I had ever heard of a Black Forest Swiss Roll was from my own mouth; I also thought it could not then be called a Swiss Roll as the Black Forest was in Germany, not Switzerland. I considered they would not notice the geographic error — a lot of people don't even know where Nottingham Forest is.

I had eaten Black Forest Gateau on numerous occasions in the seventies and had the privilege of eating a Black Forest Gateau baked by none other than Bill Findlay himself, a baker from Cullen who had worked offshore in the eighties on board the same production platform as myself. I knew then what this creation should taste like but there was no danger of me turning out something as professional as Bill would have done; he had at one stage in his career been Head Confectioner on the Cunard passenger cruise ship QE2. Although I had no chance of emulating Bill's skills, he was my inspiration for the Swiss Roll. After gathering the Kirsch, Morello Cherries and the rest of the ingredients I managed to create a reasonable representation of a Black Forest gateau, but in a roll.

I have included the picture below of the first one I made at home. A little rough admittedly but they say it is always better to leave a little room for improvement. It may interest you to note that I have not eaten a Black Forest Roll or Gateau since the Bakeoff. I finalized my recipe for the Black Forest Swiss Roll and set about dreaming up something presentable for the Showstopper recipe for thirty-six mini British cakes.

I thought long and hard about mini British cakes; Mini Victoria Sponge cakes, Dundee Cake, Mini Cherry Cakes and so it went on. There were many arguments with my better half as to what would be the most inspiring cake. After much thought and discussion, I decided on mini frangipane style cakes with homemade raspberry jelly and finished with fresh cream and raspberries. The next challenge then was to successfully bake thirty-six of these and make certain they were identical. I bought two new cake pans with twelve holes and loose bottoms, ideal for my purpose. After a bit of experimentation with ingredients I made one dozen of my intended cakes.

Almond & Raspberry Fresh Cream Cakes

The next task was to devise a 3D biscuit display with at least eight elements to it. We were told it could be a forest scene, a circus or fairground, or some similar scenario, the only stipulation was that the biscuit models had to be 3D and free standing. First, I thought about doing a biscuit Stonehenge made of shortbread but that seemed too simple, as did another idea I had for a "Sculpture Park" with Henry Moore style sculptures. The Sculpture Park would have made it easy as any "mistakes" could be put down to it actually being an abstract form. On reflection I think I would have gone for that, what I did do was a scene of Zulu fishing boats from the late nineteenth century.

I should perhaps explain why I chose the fishing boat display and more importantly why were they known as "Zulus". In 1879, William Campbell of Lossiemouth built a new style of fishing boat; he was assisted in the design of the boat by my Great Grandfather, George Stephen of W&G Stephen, Boatbuilders, Banff. W&G Stephen built wooden boats at the Greenbanks in Banff at the mouth of the River Deveron. Every year or so my Great Grandfather or his brother William, along with some of the workmen from the yard, would take a trip by sea to the Black Isle in the inner Moray Firth to cut down Scots Pine trees for the purpose of making boats masts. These would be towed back to Banff behind their boat, there to be seasoned for future use. Whilst on his way to the Black Isle on one of these expeditions in 1878 storm conditions were encountered and he had to head to Lossiemouth harbour for shelter.

They had to linger a few days in Lossiemouth whilst the storm abated and during this time, my Great Grandfather had several meetings with William Campbell at his boatyard. William had discussed with my Great Grandfather a new design for a two masted fishing boat and apparently, his contribution to the design was the steeply raked stern, which gave a longer deck with improved manoeuvrability. The design was implemented in the building of the first boat, launched at Lossiemouth in 1879 she was named "Nonesuch" but she was quite a small boat at 39 feet.

In 1879, the Zulu wars were raging in South Africa and along with the British Army engaged in this conflict were a few Scottish regiments; the Perthshire Volunteers (90th), Argyllshire Highlanders (91st), the Scotch Brigade (94th) and the Duke of Edinburgh's Lanarkshire (99th). It was known that there were some veterans of the Zulu wars who had returned to the Northeast of Scotland with tales of the strength and bravery of the Zulu Warriors. It is said that the new fishing boat built in Lossiemouth by William Campbell was likened in speed and strength to the Zulu Warrior and very soon, the name of Zulu was applied to the craft. The name must have met with approval as the craft has been known as the Zulu ever since. W&G Stephen, Banff, went on to build numerous Zulu craft at the Greenbanks, some of them reaching the length of 80 feet with a mainmast around 90 feet and a diameter at the step of over 2 feet. One of the last Zulu boats still surviving, of around 80 feet in length, was the Research built in 1903 by W&G Stephen. This fine craft is currently preserved at the Fisheries Museum in Anstruther, Fife, and the picture below shows her in her final berth, indoors. Anstruther and the Museum are well worth a visit if you are in the area, if only for the fact that the second best fish and chips in the UK are sold next door to the museum. On my last visit they were still cooking the fish in beef dripping, which adds another dimension to the taste and flavour. For arguably the best fish supper in Scotland, you need to visit my old home town and the newly refurbished Portknockie Fish and Chip shop, which has been under new management for the past two years. They do an excellent haddock and chips there and it is cooked on demand.

So it was decided that my 3D display would be a fleet of Zulu fishing boats, I just had to come up with a suitable biscuit recipe and needed to construct suitable templates. I used a sketch from a book on Zulu Craft to base my template design on but later I constructed biscuit cutters in the shapes required, using 3mm tin plate. This I thought would speed up the process of baking the biscuits at the Bakeoff as time they say is always of the essence and especially during the Bakeoff.

The signature recipe we had to produce for Week Two of the Bakeoff was a savoury biscuit suitable to serve with cheese. I initially thought of doing oatcakes but reconsidered this choice, as it did seem to entail much in the way of baking, even though oatcakes are indeed the best possible accompaniment to cheese. Still thinking along simple lines, I decided that Scottish tea or butter biscuits would be a wiser choice. In the old days in the Northeast of Scotland, these butter biscuits were sold at one farthing each and soon became known as "farthings".

The decision was made then, I would submit the farthings as my savoury biscuits. However, as suspected, Chloe thought them not complex enough, although she admitted they were attractive sounding. A compromise was reached which entailed me having to make my own butter to be served alongside the biscuits. She had tried to persuade me to do several different flavours of butter but I rebelled against that. One had to bear in mind that in the days when these biscuits were sold at a farthing each, people were lucky to have butter never mind "flavoured" butter. Week two of the Bakeoff saw me arriving with a piece of Caboc cheese to serve along with my biscuits and homemade butter. Caboc is a cream cheese originating in the Isle of Skye and is reputedly the oldest cheese in Scotland. Mine was quite new, as I had bought it at Brodie Countryfare near Forres. Incidentally, it is worth noting that after the biscuit judging had taken place, we left the tent to go to the "Green Room" for coffee. On return to the tent and eager to sample one another's bakes, there was nothing left on my bench; the crew had consumed biscuits, cheese and butter.

No sooner had I submitted my recipes for Weeks One and Two of the Bakeoff than Chloe then requested I submit, before Monday 24th March, my recipes for Weeks Three and Four. For Week Three she wanted a recipe for rye bread rolls and a recipe for a Showstopper Filled Centrepiece Loaf. The rye bread rolls were not a problem. I created a recipe based on 60-40 with 60% strong white flour and 40% rye flour. I also decided to add sultanas and caraway seeds to the mix and to finish off the top with oatmeal. A few experiments at home convinced me that the rolls were actually quite tasty (with a bit of butter). That was one recipe out of the way.

The stuffed centrepiece loaf was a different kettle of fish, although I did not experiment with fish but just about everything else. One of the first things I tried was a white bloomer loaf with a stuffing of meat loaf, although a splendid taste, it had too many air spaces around it after baking and that did not look too professional. After a few more attempts at home I finally came up with a picnic loaf with a stuffing of chicken, home-made pesto, sun dried tomato; red, green and yellow capsicum with a dusting of parmesan cheese. The stuffing rested on a layer of Parma ham to prevent any sogginess in the bottom of the loaf. The outside of the loaf was decorated with various designs in dough. This seemed to work, it looked good and had a superb taste, as it should have done with around eighteen separate ingredients.

On then to the Week 4 recipe request, this was for eight individual portion self-saucing puddings followed by the showstopper Baked Alaska. One would think that the team behind these recipe requests was trying to be as awkward as possible. Back on to the internet to try and source eight individual ovenproof dishes for the self-saucing puddings. This proved a little difficult as most of the sets were available in packs of six and I didn't really like to end up with a dozen of these dishes. I already had six small aluminium pudding basins and I experimented with these with a simple lemon sponge pudding, which created its own sauce. This was a partial success but the sauce dried out too quickly, owing I suspect to the very small size of the bowls. I had a recipe for a sticky toffee pudding with a separate part for the toffee sauce so I then set about changing the recipe so that the pudding would create its own sauce in the bottom of the dish. I successfully created such a pudding in two small bowls, which I already had in my possession. Back on to the internet then to look for eight suitable pudding basins. These I found eventually, they were the correct size and available individually so eight was not a problem.

The new pudding basins arrived in a few days and I set about baking eight at once. This was very successful and the taste was better than expected with a tasty toffee sauce appearing in the bottom of the bowl as if by magic. We were, of course, faced with the problem of eight sticky toffee puddings between the two of us. We never ate these again for a while, but at least I had another successful recipe for Chloe.

On to the Baked Alaska. As we had to make our own ice cream, it was back to the Internet to look for a budget ice cream machine. I came across the Andrew James machine at £27, ordered one and it arrived the next day courtesy of Royal Mail. This machine was simply a bowl with a paddle driven by a small electric motor. Before use, the bowl had to be placed in the deep freeze overnight. This I did and made a vanilla ice cream the following day. I like ice cream and I really liked the stuff I had made. The baked Alaska itself did not present any problems as we had made these plenty of times in the 70's and 80's.

By this time, it was Sunday 23rd March and it was with some relief that I was able to present to Chloe my recipes for Weeks Three and Four by the deadline of Monday 24th March.

I guess, like me, you feel you have had enough of Chloe's recipe requests for the moment. I think I will finish off this chapter with an old Scots recipe, based on an enriched dough for Garibaldi Scones. My father and my older brother used to make these. Although this is probably not the exact method and ingredients they would have used, they taste almost the same. At least I like to convince myself that they do. Like Garibaldi biscuits, these have dried fruit in them, in this case juicy sultanas. Have a look at this recipe then I will take you back to my schooldays and introduce you to Charlie the Clydesdale horse.

Garibaldi Scones

Ingredients

500g/1lb 2oz strong white flour

60g/2 oz caster sugar

60g/2 oz salted butter softened

2 free-range eggs

14g or ½ oz instant yeast

2 tsp salt

150ml/5fl oz warm milk

140ml/4½fl oz water

150g juicy sultanas

Method

1.Preheat the oven to 220C/425F/Gas 7.

2.To make the dough, place all the ingredients into a large bowl or a mixer with a dough hook fitted, keep aside 50ml of the water. Mix well then slowly add the remaining water as required to form a dough and knead or continue in the mixer for 6 minutes.

3.Turn the dough onto a lightly floured surface and knead well for 10 minutes or until the dough is smooth and elastic. Place the dough in a bowl, cover with cling film or a tea towel and allow to prove for one hour.

4. Once the dough has proved for one hour, knock it back and add 150g of juicy sultanas. Chuff to distribute the sultanas evenly. Divide into three pieces and roll out each piece into a circle of approx. eight inches then divide into 6 triangle shaped pieces, or 4 pieces if you like them bigger. Repeat for the other two pieces of dough and place the 18 triangles on two lined baking trays, cover and prove for one hour. Once proved, spray with an egg glaze and bake at 200 degrees C for 12 minutes or until nicely browned on top. Remove from oven and cool on wire racks.

These have a nice taste on their own and with some chilled butter they are fit for a King. Best eaten on the day but are almost as good the day after baking and are superb when toasted. They are well worth the time taken to bake them as you cannot buy these anywhere today, at least I have not seen them for sale since my brother Ian made them.

Note: To make the egg glaze, beat one egg and add a pinch of salt and two teaspoons water before passing through a sieve to remove the chalaza. Pour the resulting liquid into your spray container.

CHAPTER SIX – 1954

When I was Seven

Right arm in a sling, I spent the rest of the summer holidays enjoying the sunshine. When I look back on those days, it seems to me that the sun did shine all day, every day. I was given a small plastic golf club and ball and used an empty can to make a hole in the lawn at the side of the house. What you do is place the open end of the can onto the grass, and then hammer it down to the depth of the can, removing the chunk of grass & earth with the can. After removing the chunk of grass from inside the can, invert it and knock it down the depth of the hole. Then you have a perfect hole for a putting green and days of amusement. I became somewhat of an expert at single-handed putting and carried on with that style, even after I had had the plaster removed. Just like Nelson, I had to carry on left-handedly because when they removed the plaster my arm remained at ninety degrees. I had been back at school for a few weeks before it eventually straightened out. I say straightened out because it looked like it had from one angle, unfortunately from the side it had a distinct lump and bend at the elbow. I do recall a neighbour suggesting that I carry buckets of coal etc. into the house, to aid in the strengthening and straightening of my limb, but I never fell for that.

I can recall making a trip back to the hospital with my Mother where she enquired of the doctor there as to when the arm would return to normal. He said not to worry, as it would straighten out as I grew up. It never did and is still as bent as it was. The arm however has remained as strong and as useful as anyone could wish an arm to be; at the age of seventy-two, I still have suffered no pain from the old injury. One can only notice the deformed elbow when I straighten out my arm, some people do not like the look of it, but most of the time it remains un-noticed and has done everything that I have required of my right arm.

It wasn't long before I was equipped with new shoes and clothes and returned, accompanied by my still bent arm, to continue my education in Miss Watson's class. On Sunday, I took my two pennies to Sunday School ready to present to Jesus, but first I had to face the wrath of Miss

Donaldson who had been told the whole story behind my absence from her Sunday School class. I did not get a prize for perfect attendance that year but funnily enough got one the following year, it was a small novel entitled "Come To Tea With Me" by Montague Goodman. I do not think I ever read it as we were into the "William" books by Richmael Crompton at the time, of which series the local library located in the school was well stocked.

The family picture below from 1955 should have contained my older brother David who would have been fifteen but sadly died in 1943.

Ma 'n Pa with Ian & Sybil. Robert is on my right next to my bent arm

Opposite Summerton where we lived was a large field where the local farmer Alex Legge kept his two Clydesdale horses, Jimmy and Charlie. Jimmy was not a horse you would want to get too close to, at least we kids had managed to find out he was a bit intolerant of our company, so we depended on Charlie for much of our amusement and play. Charlie was enormous and could easily hold four of us eight year olds on his back at the same time and then walk round the circumference of the field. We liked Charlie and I think the feeling was mutual. As you know, my father kept hens and pigs and any leftover bread that could not be sold was normally fed to them. It was easy for us then to grab some old loaves before heading out to see Charlie. That is why Charlie was always pleased to see us; he also knew what was good for him, as he would normally eat all the brown bread first before starting on the white. Charlie carried out all the duties required of a farm horse and in addition had a part-time job pulling the Portknockie Town Council dustcart on a weekly basis. On "bucket days", Charlie would be hitched to an old farm cart and pull it round the village collecting the rubbish – mainly ashes from the fireplaces in those days.

No recycling, apart from the fact that ashes were occasionally employed in surfacing the local pathways, a splendid idea as this prevented the paths becoming muddy when it rained. Unfortunately, the ashes are missing today; it is all too easy, during wet weather, to arrive home "clarted in dubs". *(covered in mud)*

Charlie the horse was to achieve fame on a worldwide basis, when he refused to pull the new dustcart, which the Town Council had spent £300 pounds on acquiring early in 1954. The problem was that the new cart was a great deal bigger and heavier than the old farm cart that Charlie had been pulling for years, and he would not or could not pull the new one. Portknockie Town Council decided then to sell the cart; it was either that or invest more of the ratepayer's money in a tractor to replace Charlie. The horse was owned by local farmer Alex Legge who had served with the Gordon Highlanders, during the war in Italy amongst other places. Until the day he retired through ill health, Alex wore his army webbing belt round the waist of his dungarees. The only time you ever saw Alex without the belt was at the bowling green, enjoying a game of bowls, or when he was on duty as a "Special Constable", a position in which he served for many years in Portknockie. Apparently, Alex finally had a word with Charlie; the horse relented and started pulling the cart again.

It may have been that Alex had bribed Charlie with extra feed if he carried on pulling the dust-cart, anyway Charlie continued in his post until Christmas 1955. Before that, in October 1955, Alex had requested an increase in the hire charge for Charlie to £3.00 from the current £2-2/6d weekly fee. This was regarded by the Council as exorbitant and they offered £2-10/- which was accepted. They did not have to pay this increased fee for very long, as Charlie was finally made redundant from his Council work on Christmas Eve 1955, when he was replaced by a tractor costing £600. Charlie carried on working on the farm and pulling Alex's "Tattie Cairt" around the village on Saturdays. As I indicated earlier, this story of Charlie and the dustcart spread round the world, and was reported in the press as far away as Australia. The local paper in Buckie also took up the story when "Spike", writing in the "Buckie Squeak", composed a short tongue-in-cheek article regarding Charlie. This story centred on Portknockie Town Council and their inability to recruit sufficient volunteers to populate the Council Chambers once a month. The Council decided that as the horse had recently been made redundant, he might be willing to become a Council member. A delegation was then sent to interview the horse; inducements were offered to Charlie, consisting of a bag of oats at every Council meeting plus convenorship of the Cleansing Department, thus giving the horse total control of tractor operations. Charlie refused, indicating that he would settle for nothing less than the post of Provost. The Council then abandoned their plans for the horse and looked at alternative ways of increasing recruitment. It is remarkable to note that serving one's community in those days was done on a purely voluntary basis. This is in direct contrast to the situation we have today, when local councillors are rewarded with an annual salary plus expenses for their efforts.

Throughout 1954 I continued to enjoy being back at school and I must add that I relished the additional sympathetic treatment I received from Miss Watson, having been injured and consigned to hospital for part of the summer. Despite enjoying school, the highlight of the day was always running home at 3.45 and changing into my "playing out" clothes. In those days there was very little that would persuade us to spend any time at all indoors, unless absolutely necessary, like meal times and having to go to bed. Saturday night was when we always had to have a bath, an unnecessary exercise as far as we were concerned. You can imagine our joy then when "Uncle" Bob Mitchell, who visited us with his wife Anita from time to time, had said he had read an article saying that excessive bathing was bad for the skin.

Despite Bob's sincerity, my mother continued to have us scrubbed on a weekly basis, on a Saturday night, all ready for Sunday School. Anita, who was a cousin of my father's, lived with Bob on Deeside and we visited them from time to time; always a great experience for us, mainly due to the fact that Anita made the finest meat loaf we'd ever tasted. My mother's meat loaf was good but Anita's was on another level. Bob was employed as a gardener and handyman, I think Bob had missed his vocation as he was always interested in what you were doing and ready to help where he could; like all pipe smokers he had a very patient outlook and thoughtful demeanour, he would have made a great teacher. Another relative of dad's who visited us from time to time was Auntie Adeline with her daughter and grandchildren. Not exactly sure why, but the children had to have a bath, not just every week, but every night! They had my sympathy. My mother did not think much of the practice either, what was this doing to the household demand for hot water, not to mention the electricity bill. That was how our summers were punctuated, every week or so another relative would arrive for a free holiday. Looking back it must have meant a great deal of extra work for my mother, as she had a six bedroomed house to look after in addition to decorating cakes and completing the accounts for the bakery. On top of all that, she was saddled with Robert and me and had to cook three meals a day, not just for the family but also for whoever happened to be staying with us at the time. Summer time in Portknockie was a time when the population increased, especially during the Glasgow Fair fortnight when the trains on the Saturday would discharge hundreds of Glaswegians all along the coast. In addition to the village filling up, two of the nearby farms, Cruats & Hillhead, would play host to the Boys Brigade Camps. We had two companies arrive in Portknockie each year, the 141 and the 278 Glasgow BB. They set up camp in the local farmer's fields, along with large marquee tents for dining and assembly.

A large number of householders in Portknockie played host to families from Glasgow looking for budget accommodation during the Fair Fortnight. Most of the people in Portknockie were glad of the wee bit extra cash, whilst the Glaswegians enjoyed a cheaper holiday than would otherwise have been possible in Blackpool and other more exotic locations. We got the Macmillan's. The Macmillan's were a very nice family, five of them, Mr & Mrs Macmillan, their son and two daughters. They arrived in their Hillman car along with what seemed like the rest of Glasgow's population on the first Saturday of the Glasgow Fair and played golf, all five of them, for a fortnight. They would however have a few afternoons on the beach, but it was mainly golf with them. Mrs Macmillan was a teacher and her husband some kind of civil servant I believe. The only other Macmillan I'd heard of at the time was Harold Macmillan, a member of Churchill's cabinet who was later to become Prime Minister. I was convinced he was related somehow to our Mr Macmillan.

Today, most Scots will travel to Spain, Greece and Turkey or just about anywhere with sunshine and cheap beer, leaving the northeast of Scotland in peace. I do not know where the Boys Brigade from Glasgow go these days but it is certainly not to Portknockie. The local population I am sure miss the Boys Brigade arriving each summer for their camp; the highlight of the week was when they would march, together with their bagpipes, to church on Sunday. The 278 Glasgow Company of Boys Brigade held their camp at Denside farm up until 1971; then at Cruats Farm from 1972 to 1988 when they started to go somewhere else, they have not been seen back in Portknockie since. Similarly, the 141 Glasgow BB, who camped annually at Hillhead Farm, like the Ninth Legion have not been heard of for a long time.

Portknockie in 1954 did not have a Boys Brigade Company; instead, we had the cubs and scouts. The cubs and scouts were led by Mr Jackie Taylor, who had served with distinction during the war with the Gordon Highlanders and been awarded, along with other decorations, the Military Medal. I first met Jackie when I was around three years old when he was working for my father driving the horse-drawn bakery van. I recall that as being one of my earliest memories, coming up Park Street Portknockie, sitting next to Jackie on the horse van. I did not get to join the cubs that year, as I had to wait until I was eight, but more of that later.

Meanwhile, back at school we continued to enjoy being in Miss Watson's class, one of the weekly highlights being physical education on the radio. On Thursday mornings at ten o'clock, we gathered in the school hall with our gym shoes and had half an hour of "knob drill", our nickname for this weekly activity. Kenneth had christened it "knob drill", the theory being I think that a knob on the wireless had to be turned to initiate the session. Later on, we had Mrs Christie as a "drill teacher", she spent a lot of time I recall, lecturing us on personal hygiene and convincing us we had to wash our hands after being to the toilet. The outbreak of typhoid fever and later the polio epidemic were the main reasons for the increased hand washing. Up until then I had thought you only needed to wash your hands if you had pissed on them.

Time now I think for another recipe. It was usually a Wednesday and a winter Wednesday at that, when we had lentil soup at home and half a loaf of bread along with it. I still enjoy lentil soup today and we have it quite frequently. It is cheap, very nourishing and if you can also make your own homemade bread to accompany the soup, you will have something to warm the cockles of your heart.

Ingredients

125g red lentils

3 large carrots

100g swede

1 medium onion finely chopped

500ml chicken or vegetable stock

1 litre water

30g butter or 30ml vegetable oil

Salt & pepper to taste

Method

Melt the butter in a large saucepan and sauté the onion until soft and translucent.

Clean the carrots and grate two of them, chopping the other into small dice.

Chop the swede into similar sized pieces.

Add the stock, water, lentils, carrots and swede to the saucepan and season lightly before bringing to the boil and simmering for 40 minutes or until the carrots are soft and the lentils have separated.

Today they sometimes have this soup with coriander in it, but we had none of that in the garden when I was a boy.

When cooked serve with slices of home-baked bloomer, the recipe for which is very easy and follows.

Wholemeal Bloomer

Ingredients

300g strong white flour

200g strong wholemeal flour

40ml vegetable oil or 30g very soft butter

300 ml cold water

10g salt

10g active dried yeast

Add all the ingredients to a large bowl, initially keeping the salt and yeast on different sides of the bowl. Mix well and knead on a floured board for around 10 minutes until smooth and elastic. Return the dough to the bowl, cover and leave to prove in the warmth of your kitchen for one to two hours. It should double in size, so when it does, remove from the bowl and knock it back. Shape the dough on your baking tray to a sausage shape, cover and leave to rise for one hour. When the second prove is complete, spray the dough with water and sprinkle with a little wholemeal flour before making a few slashes with a razor blade on top. Place in a hot oven at around 220 degrees C and bake for around 30 minutes. Cool on a wire rack and sit back for a minute or so to appreciate the lovely aroma in your kitchen. Make this in the morning so that it will be cool enough to eat with the lentil soup at lunchtime.

CHAPTER SEVEN

More Recipes

Saint Patrick's Day dawned with no sign of a pint of Guinness, instead I received from Chloe the recipe requests for weeks five and six of the Bakeoff; the deadline being set for Monday 31st March.

Week five of the Bakeoff was Pies and Tarts week and the request was for a Signature bake of a set custard tart, whilst the Showstopper called for a tower of pies, at least three pies in the tower. First of all I thought I'd make it easy for myself and do a tower of three hot water crust pies with a pork filling and add to each one a different flavour or additional ingredient. Then I had to devise a method of presenting the pies in a tower format. It was off to the shed to prepare the clay for the construction of my tower.

Once I had prepared my clay and completed the design for the tower supports I then set about experimenting in the kitchen, trying out my pie recipes. Having seriously considered the hot water crust pork pies I had planned on, I decided that Chloe and the Hollyberry might well dismiss these as being too simple. I came up with the idea of doing three different types of pastry, with three different types of pie filling. What I decided on was a steak and vegetable pie in rough puff pastry for the bottom pie and a haddock in cheese sauce with puff pastry in the middle. To crown it all a lemon meringue pie with pate sucre. The sizes I decided would be large, medium and small from the bottom up, the bottom pie being on a stand with suitable supports for the other pies. The whole ensemble was christened "The Pieffel Tower" and at the time of conception I considered this a pie of some pedigree and would make me a sure-fire candidate for the Star Baker accolade... dream on Norman!

Having successfully experimented with my pie recipes I then returned to the shed and completed the stand and supports for the presentation of The Pieffel Tower. By the time of the pie recipe deadline, the tower supports were finished, fired and glazed. Back to the kitchen to have a go at the Signature bake, the set custard tart. I had it in mind to keep the Signature bake straightforward and just do a tarte au citron, a simple lemon tart. I had baked a few of these at home and they turned out impeccably.

On then to the recipes for week six of the Bakeoff. The Signature bake was for a European Style Yeast-Leavened Cake with the Showstopper demand being for a Tiered Dobos Torte, a minimum of two tiers with a stated emphasis on elaborate sugar work and decoration. *(You can see at this point that things are getting easier)*

Orange and Raspberry Savarin Yeasted Cake

The yeast-leavened cake was no problem at all, I'd made quite a few of these in my time and decided to bake an orange flavoured cake; baked in a savarin mould, soaked in orange syrup with orange liqueur and finished off with fresh cream and raspberries. I baked one at home just to check out the recipe and it turned out magnificently with a very tasty moist flavour, most definitely the correct choice. I had included a goodly splash of the orange liqueur so was convinced this would go down well with Mary. Encouraged by my success with the yeasted cake I then set about attempting to find out just what a Doboz Torte was. I found the Doboz Torte description on the internet. It was also on page 155 of Mary Berry's Baking Bible – The Hungarian

Doboz Torte. Between the internet and Mary's recipe, I devised my own version of the Doboz Torte. A few days and one or two burnt fingers later I managed to construct something that resembled a work of art; perhaps more abstract than fine art, but a fine looking creation nonetheless.

The Dobos Torte MkI

In retrospect, my Dobos Torte had about it the appearance of an oil-drilling rig; however, I was very pleased with my creation and overjoyed to rediscover the healing powers of ice-cold water on my burnt fingers. Someone told me later that there are special sugar craft gloves available that go a long way toward the prevention of blisters. With a bit more refinement I managed to convince myself (*not however Mrs C*) that I had a potential Showstopper on my hands.

Monday 31st March arrived with much celebration on my part as I had once more managed to submit my recipes before the deadline. These then had to withstand an interrogation by Chloe later in the week. Yes, just when you thought you had it all sown up, somebody else would come along and rip it all to bits. Meantime, we had already received the recipe requests for weeks seven and eight of the Bakeoff.

By this time, we were getting a bit 'over-sugared' and longing for something savoury to bake. We got our request in the shape of a demand for a recipe for week seven, Signature Savoury Parcels. This was indeed a refreshing alternative to all the sugar work of the previous week. Joy was short-lived as the Showstopper bake was for twenty-four éclairs. I suppose that in retrospect we could have made savoury éclairs; there was nothing in the request that said we could not. Perhaps a chicken and sun dried tomato éclair adorned with pesto and a dusting of parmesan would have impressed the Hollyberry, but we will never know. Like in an examination, always read the question!

I put the thinking cap on again,(*I've got one I bought in Holland a few years back but never had much use for it.*) What I eventually came up with was prawn and crab parcels, wrapped in filo pastry and deep-fried, to be served with a sweet chilli sauce. The only snag was I would have to learn how to make my own filo pastry. No chef or baker would make his or her own filo, rather it would be shop bought. This was the Bakeoff, however, and I would have to make my own.

This task turned out to be a lot easier than I thought; I would say that patience was the most important ingredient here and it was not long before I had this down to a fine art. There are excellent tuition videos on YouTube that assist greatly. This was a godsend to me, as we have no professional filo makers in the Buckie area. Looking back, I could have visited Stoke Newington, which has an abundance of small bakeries selling Baklava so I may have been able to pick their brains if I had lived in London.

On to the request for the eclairs recipe; twenty-four in all, of a uniform size with inventive flavours and exciting decorative toppings. Ever get the feeling that they are barking up the wrong tree? What I came up with was twelve eclairs with a crème patisserie filling finished with coffee flavour fondant and a piped dark chocolate design. My second dozen were to be cream filled with elaborate chocolate decorations atop a chocolate fondant coating.

The raspberry and cream Savarin I planned for the Week 6 yeasted cake Signature Bake turned out to be one of the best cakes I have ever tasted and so I include the recipe here. Even if you have to go out and buy a Savarin mould or Bundt tin it's worth it; try TK Maxx as they always appear to stock a wide range of economically priced bakeware, ring moulds included.

Orange & Raspberry Savarin Cake

Ingredients

50ml milk

8g dried active quick yeast

200g plain flour

100g unsalted butter

3 eggs

325g sugar

500 ml water

zest of one orange

75ml Cointreau orange liqueur

300ml double cream

300g raspberries

Method

Add the yeast to the milk and leave for 15-20 minutes until frothing

Mix the flour, yeast and eggs in a bowl, cover and leave to rise (45-60 minutes).

After dough has risen, add the butter and 2 tbsp. sugar to the dough and mix well.

Transfer the mixture to your Savarin ring and allow to prove for 40 minutes before baking at 190 C for 30 minutes.

Boil the water with the remaining sugar plus the orange rind and simmer for around 10 minutes. Stir the Cointreau into the syrup and pour over the cake while still in the mould.

When cake has cooled, remove from the mould and decorate with whipped double cream, you will need about 600ml and decorate with fresh raspberries.

CHAPTER EIGHT

Now Eight I Join The Cubs

Easter 1955 found me heading for my eighth birthday in June; this is when I left the comfort of Miss Watson's and with heavy heart headed down the hall to Miss Rottweiler's classroom. She had a formidable reputation and most of her ex pupils will probably shudder at the mention of her name; more than a few would have had her burned as a witch, those among the more forgiving. She was a fine example of the old Scots Presbyterian attitude to education; she would literally hammer facts into your head. I do not think that we learned a great deal under Miss Rottweiler, most of the time we were too frightened. The only thing I can recall from being in her class was learning long division of pounds, shillings and pence; including halfpennies and farthings. Even today, there are ex pupils from her later years at Portknockie primary, voicing curses on her via Facebook. I believe she is still alive and under guard in an old folks home; the exact location of which is being kept secret.

Arriving at the age of eight years resulted in me developing three distinct memories from that time in my life. The birthday itself was very memorable as I received from Mam & Dad a copy of the "Boys Book of Heroes", which I read cover to cover on many occasions. One particular sketch showed Michael Faraday in his laboratory, in the midst of a cloud of broken glass and smoke; the caption read, "One day there was a terrific explosion". Another memorable illustration was of Sgt Hollister VC climbing on to the turret of a German tank with a grenade in his hand. The amazing coincidence here was that many years later, I recall being in my early fifties at the time, I met Sgt.Hollister's grandson. The second important point about being eight was that I was now eligible to join the Cub Scouts. I was looking forward very much to the end of the summer holidays when I would be joining the Cubs. Not that I was particularly keen on the Cubs but was very keen on the Scouts as they got to go off on a camp each year; living in tents and lighting fires to cook on. Lighting fires brings to mind the third significance of being eight years old; I had reached the age (or so they said later) of criminal responsibility.

After another long and seemingly unending summer break, it was back to school in August. More importantly the following week I joined the Cubs, the 1st Portknockie Pack. I got a navy gansey and a cub cap from McKay's in Buckie. I had two things sown on to the gansey, the tab "1st Portknockie" and a red triangle signifying my membership of the "Reds". There was plenty room on the gansey for all the badges I thought I would get, unfortunately that ambition remained unfulfilled. In order to qualify to take the tests for the various badge awards, such as Arts and Crafts, First Aid, Woodcraft and other skills, one had to first of all pass the "Tenderfoot" stage. I cannot recall exactly what was required to qualify for the two Tenderfoot badges (one for the cap and one for the gansey); the only thing I know for sure was that I was unable to qualify, despite numerous tests. Jackie Taylor, who led the Cubs, must have given up in exasperation; I was never able to recite the Cub Scout promise among other requirements. It is perhaps significant that I never bothered to find out what dyb dyb dyb and dob dob dob meant until I was in my fifties; that was a Eureka moment. It is *do your best* and *do our best* for those of you who do not know. If I joined the Cubs today, I would probably be fast-tracked to the rank of Sixer.

As a Wolf Cub, my gansey remained bereft of badges until I was ten years old, when I had to part company with the Cubs. My mother, you see, was an accomplished seamstress and had made me a new pair of shorts. She could have taught the World how to conserve and recycle; an old blanket bearing the wartime utility mark supplied the material. They looked vaguely like tweed, having a herringbone style pattern, and although they were longer than usual, it was in these shorts that I proudly set off for the Cub meeting hall one winter evening in November 1957. Unfortunately, entry was refused, the reason being that they were the wrong colour and too long. I went round the corner of the Cub meeting hall and folded up the legs. I made another attempt at entry, but was turned away once more, the regulation being grey or dark coloured shorts, two inches above the knee. I am not too sure what happened after that but it involved some kind of heated exchange between my Mother and one of the Cub leaders. The result was that the Cubs and I parted company, which was a real disappointment as I had been keen on trying to join the Scouts the following year. I was not quite sure if I would have been able to join the Scouts with me not qualifying as a Cub, but there was me thinking I might have given it a go anyway.

As a small boy in Portknockie, one of my favourite times of the year was bonfire night; the fifth of November, Guy Fawkes Night. 1955 saw Portknockie with an early bonfire, one of its biggest in living memory. A real fire; not just a lum on fire or a misbehaving chip pan but a blaze of epic proportions. This was when Alex Legge's cornyard, where the fruits of the year's harvest were stacked, took on fire. I say took on fire but it wasn't spontaneous combustion; there had been an arsonist afoot and it involved the deployment of three appliances from the Fire Service, providing unexpected Saturday afternoon entertainment for almost the entire population of the village. You can tell by my language that I've had conversations with firemen or firefighters as they're now known; only the uninitiated call them fire engines, those in the know refer to them as appliances and of course most of these appliances are called "Dennis".

It was a Saturday afternoon, in late autumn, a bit overcast and there was a light drizzle. Three pals and myself had been wandering round the streets, looking for something to occupy us for the rest of the day. One of this gang of four had been the recipient of a sixpence that morning, a gift from his Auntie, so as a diversion we wandered off to Georgie Kingies shop; some liquorice sticks and caramels were bought, along with a box of matches. Sucking the liquorice, we headed for the railway station, in the hope that the signalman would allow us into the signal box. The reason being that there was always a nice fire burning and it was a chance to dry out and get warm for a bit. This Saturday, however, we found the signalman to be a total stranger, the usual one was on holiday and this fella would not let us near the box. We decided instead to head for the big shed in the garden of Summerton, where we would get a bit of shelter from the rain. Unfortunately, on the way there we passed Alex Legge's cornyard where we decided to take shelter from the rain. The youngest of the group and owner of the matches had got a bit of a soaking from the rain and decided to start a small fire near where the bales of straw were stacked. This small fire got out of control very quickly and we all decided to vacate the scene. I ran home and the others went off in the direction of the harbour.

I watched the blaze take hold from my bedroom window in Summerton. I then made a huge mistake; I decided to run down into the village and tell Alex Legge that his cornyard was on fire. I had just gone over the railway bridge when I was grabbed by a policeman, Mr Parris the local bobby, who enquired as to where I was off to in such a rush. I explained what had happened and all he said was, "I think you'll be coming with me" and took hold of my arm as we marched back up over the railway bridge and onwards to Summerton. By this time a large crowd had gathered at the scene of the fire and they all turned and looked as I was marched toward Summerton under the grip of Mr Parris, he might as well have had me in cuffs.

In later years, my Dad eventually bought a television set, a 17" Ultra in a shiny walnut cabinet. One of the programmes which I watched avidly, was Dixon of Dock Green, and that was when I decided that I would like to make the police force my career. However, I think this little episode put paid to that ambition and I never grew tall enough, unlike today when they concentrate on intelligence rather physical size. Parris assumed that he had just apprehended an arsonist and demanded to know who my accomplices were. By this time, we were in the sitting room in Summerton with my mother and father and I confessed to them who I had been playing out with, trying to tell them, I was not guilty of starting the fire. Parris then tried to scare me by saying I could be committed to borstal and, he succeeded, not in committing me to borstal but in scaring me and that stayed with me for years afterwards.

I was then despatched to my room where I had a grandstand view of the fire. The inferno at this time was in its early stages and only one fire appliance was present, the one from Cullen. The unit from Buckie arrived soon after. Later the part time firemen from Fochabers were requested to attend. The intensity of the blaze was such that the hydrant points in the vicinity were unable to cope with the demand and they had to run about five hundred feet of hose to the dam at Cruats Farm. By the time of the arrival of the third appliance, the assembled crowd of spectators had grown to what looked like in excess of five hundred souls. What really stuck in my head was seeing my Mam crying in the bedroom but my Dad didn't seem to be too bothered by the whole episode. My Mam that day, head in hands and sobbing her heart out had a profound effect on me and I made my mind up to try and be "good" but I was always getting into some scrape or another, usually through fault of my own.

The main blaze was extinguished by early evening, although the fire continued to smoulder until Monday morning. This made the day of one of the little gobshites in my class, who raised his hand and said to Miss Rottweiler - this was at nine, not ten or lunchtime but straight away, first thing in the morning - he could not wait to get the teacher told. "Please Miss; the fire that Norman Calder started on Saturday is still burning". This prompted an answering tirade from the teacher who said; "You should be feeling black burning shame after such a heinous act", and added that I would be lucky if I was ever again allowed outside to play. I protested that it wasn't me who had started the fire but that fell on deaf ears. Perhaps the worst of the punishments I received as a result of the fire was having my Meccano set locked away and I didn't get to play with it for some considerable time. By Christmas the fire was a distant memory and I had my Meccano set back in my hands, when I got a present of the Meccano accessory set 3a which made my size 3, a size 4. The icing on the cake was the Meccano clockwork motor which was also in my stocking.

In late 1955 in the Northeast of Scotland, and Banffshire in particular, a new world opened up; this was the world of television, soon to become the social pariah Lord Reith had forecast in the thirties. We did not appreciate that foresight in the fifties and could not wait until the day dawned when we could all have a television set at home. My first glimpse of live television was in Banff around mid-October 1955. My Dad had driven to Aberdeen, taking me and my brother Robert with him. On the way back in the late afternoon, we had stopped for a bag of chips in Banff. We were in my Dad's old 1937 Rolls Royce and stopped just outside the Fife Arms Hotel in the main street. The door attendant of the hotel then opened the rear door and Robert and me jumped out and ran across the road to the chip shop. It looked like the doorman was treating us as potential customers but on this occasion he was sadly mistaken. Having got our bag of chips, our attention was drawn to the small gathering at the shop a couple of doors along the street. Popping along for a look, we caught site of the first television pictures we had ever seen. The programme being broadcast was The Freddie Mills Keep Fit Show, it was almost unbelievable so we ran back to get Dad from the car. He came and had a look, saw the price of the set on display and immediately vowed he would never waste that amount of money on a wooden box; "Ye could buy a hoose for that" was his exclamation. Obviously, we were bitterly disappointed by this revelation but very much aware that the next step would be to convince our Mam that every home should have a television set.

Not a lot of people today have heard of Freddie Mills, he had been the British Light Heavy-weight boxing champion in 1950 and after his retirement from professional boxing, became a nightclub owner in London; he was one of the early television celebrities. Freddie at one time was a presenter on the BBC's first "pop" programme, The Six-Five Special, in addition to doing his keep fit programme. He was found dead in his car, shot in the head in July 1965, at the rear of his nightclub in London. When we eventually got a television set at home, I have no recollection of seeing Freddie on The Six-Five Special but do recall that first sight of a television in Banff and the Freddie Mills Keep Fit Show. Famously, Pete Murray was the presenter I remember from the Six Five Special, along with Don Lang and his Frantic Five and Laurie London singing "He's Got The Whole World in His Hands".

In 1955 television had still to arrive in Summerton, so for the moment we had to content ourselves with the wireless, Dick Barton on the BBC and Dan Dare on Radio Luxembourg. Also broadcast by Radio Luxembourg from 1952 was a re-hash of the pre-war radio show The Ovaltinies, the presidents of the new Ovaltinies Club being none other than Morecambe & Wise, later to become one of the biggest attractions ever on BBC Television.

 Television at home remained a distant vision, our main concern early in 1956 being our impending transfer to the next class at school, Primary 5 and the evil Miss Bagwart. Miss Bagwart's class was the most feared at school, worse than Miss Rottweiler's was but not as bad as the school's dental van. Once a year a huge white van would appear and take up residence in the school playground. We could tolerate the white van but not the man inside it. This was Mr Rustbucket, with a mouthful of teeth like ruined wall and breath like a badgers bum, who used his size ten boots to great effect in powering his foot operated drill. When the turn came round for someone in your class to visit the van, there would be a knock on the classroom door and a young lady, dressed in a white overall and carrying a clipboard, would appear. The class reacted with a sharp intake of breath, followed by an electric silence, until the name was called out of the next child to go to the van. Then all you could hear was a collective sigh of relief, apart from the victim who was now shitting him/herself.

We will leave the school dentist, Miss Bagwart and 1956 alone for the moment and have a look at the first week of the Great British Bakeoff and our introduction to the "Tent". Before we go on to the Bakeoff here is a recipe from my childhood, which is still a firm family favourite. My brother Robert and me used to make this quite often (if Mother was out shopping or working). It is for the old Scottish favourite – tablet. This recipe I got from a lady who came to visit my mother, I forget her name but she was something to do with the "rural" (the Scottish WI). It is the only recipe for tablet I have seen that includes custard powder. Try it, it is superb! We first made this when I was 9 years old, be careful you do not burn yourself. Boiling sugar is very hot and it sticks like shit to a blanket! Do not spoil it by adding vanilla essence; it is supposed to taste of butter and sugar and is fine that way, you will find that the custard powder gives it a unique and subtle flavour.

Ingredients

500g granulated sugar

2 tablespoons custard powder

65g butter

1 large tin Carnation evaporated milk (around 350ml)

Method

Grease a baking tin of around 20 x 30cm- size not too important.

In a large stout bottomed saucepan add the sugar and custard powder and mix thoroughly. Add the butter and evaporated milk and mix well before bringing to the boil. Simmer for around 20-25 minutes until the mix starts to colour and thicken. Once this stage is reached, remove from the heat and beat well for around 15 minutes. When you see it start to thicken significantly, pour the mix into the greased tin, leave to cool then mark into squares before turning out and eating. If you make a mistake first time you make this, recovery is easy, if it does not set properly just pop it back in the saucepan and reboil and beat it for a while longer. You will quickly recognise when the correct consistency has been reached. Of course, the reverse can happen when you beat it for too long and it starts to set in the pan.

CHAPTER NINE

Off To The Tent

The first of May saw my initial call sheet arrive from Simon at Love Productions. My flight had been booked from Inverness to Gatwick for the early afternoon on the first. I left my car at the short stay park at Inverness Airport and had an uneventful journey to Gatwick where I got the Express to Victoria, underground to Paddington then on to Newbury via Reading. Speculation was still rife in my mind as to the exact location of the Bakeoff Tent. We knew it was not going to be in its previous location near Bristol and could only assume it was near Newbury. Having studied the maps the only possible location I could come up with was Highclere Castle, the location for the Downton Abbey television series. Tonight I thought I'd find out for sure as they would be certain to let us know where we were going.

The Prezzo Restaurant in Newbury had been selected as the meeting place for all the bakers at 7.30 that evening, I had intended to get a taxi from Newbury Railway Station to the Restaurant but Murray Grindon, our chaperone, met me at the station and we walked the short distance to the Prezzo. There I finally met my fellow competitors, initially thinking, "What a rum-looking crew they are". However, I am pleased to say that first impressions are not always correct as they proved themselves over the next few weeks to be a fantastic group of human beings. I thought to myself; looks like I am the oldest one here, until Diana revealed she was retired and beat me by a year or two. The youngest was Martha at seventeen and still at school and we had a wide range of ages and backgrounds in between. What never crossed my mind at this point was the thought that one of us would be saying goodbye after two days; this was yet to come. We tried to persuade Murray to let us know the location of the "Tent" but no information on that subject was forthcoming, we would just have to wait until the following morning. The most striking looking amongst us was Iain who had a red beard and a massive outcrop of red hair standing up on his head. With him being an Irishman, I thought he could well have passed for Jedwards Dad.

At 10pm, a mini-bus appeared and drove us the five miles or so to the Hotel Mercure, Elcot Park, a conveniently located hotel in the middle of nowhere, around five miles from Newbury. Elcot Park had been the family home at one time of the great English Romantic Poet, Percy Shelley, although I doubt that Shelley would have had to cough up four quid for a pint in those days. We did not of course do much in the way of drinking at the Mercure and even less eating. We were to be collected in the morning at 6.20am – unfortunately for me I had forgotten during my retirement that there were two six o'clocks. No breakfast in the hotel, you could not really expect any of the staff to arise at such an ungodly hour to feed us. On reflection, we should have just demanded breakfast but we had not yet developed the diva mentality. Incidentally, Percy Shelley's widow was Mary Shelley, the writer and creator of Frankenstein. After Percy's death from drowning in the Meddie when his yacht sank in a storm, his heart was removed and sent to England, later ending up in a grave in Bournemouth alongside Mary. Although there is a pub in Bournemouth named the Mary Shelley, no such honour has yet been bestowed on Percy in Bournemouth. However, The Mercure Elcot Park now has a Percy Shelley Suite, refurbished whilst the Bakeoff gang were staying there. By the way, the Mary Shelley is the best of the three Weatherspoon's pubs in Bournemouth; I have had a pint and an excellent meal there.

At 6.20am, two taxis collected us and drove to the Bakeoff location. A third taxi had to be organised for Luis as he had brought all his own "gear" in a trailer with his car from Manchester. Luis had a huge suitcase, toolbox, two holdall bags, a manbag and numerous other bits and pieces. He had the biggest blowtorch I've come across, it was of industrial size and could brown off meringue in seconds. Our arrival ten minutes later at Welford Park solved the mystery. This was the location of a magnificent Georgian building, the grounds of which were the temporary home to the Great British Bakeoff Tent. I had hoped to be able to call Iris at home and say I was staying at Highclere Castle (Downton Abbey), but Welford Park was a magnificent location in its own right and I think we were all impressed with the chosen venue. Breakfast was in the form of a cold bacon roll, tea or coffee and some packets of cereals for the more adventurous. All this in the "Green Room", an annexe to the main house, which was to be our waiting room for the duration of the Bakeoff experience, when we were not in the tent that is.

Murray collected all our mobile phones and cameras, promising their return at the end of the day. Prior to our introduction to the tent, we received the compulsory health and safety briefing, then were shown the fire exits and toilet locations. It was not too far to the tent and we marched there from the front of the house in two columns of six. This was it then, we had seen it on the television screen but nothing could have prepared us for the thrill of seeing it for real. It was set in a magnificent location, surrounded by trees and in the grounds of the big house. What strikes you most is the amount of people in the tent, I think altogether there was around fifty, composed of producers, camera crew, home economists, the director and the lady who did all the washing up. There was no sign of the Hollyberry, Mel and Sue, they would arrive later by limo and park themselves in the big house itself. After a cup of coffee we marched off to the tent, it was just as you see it on the telly and for us a surreal experience. Murray showed us in and we went to our respective workstations. My position was at the front on the left hand side, just where you would not want to be on the first day. However, they said this would change randomly every week, assuming one lasted more than the first week.

We had no idea when we would have to start baking; the purpose of this visit to the tent was for us to check the supplied ingredients against our recipes. Once we had all the stuff checked out, we returned to the Green Room for another cup of coffee. Many of the twelve at this point were in awe of the occasion and still trying to figure out why they were taking part in the Bakeoff, none more than yours truly. We had just finished the coffee when the order came to assemble at the front of the house, around two hundred metres from the entrance to the tent. The camera crews appeared to be all ready and waiting for us and we marched, two abreast into the tent, onward to our workstations, removed our coats and donned our Bakeoff aprons. This was television, of course, and we had to do it all again – three times.

At this point, "Brighty"- Matthew Bright the Floor Manager - introduced himself; he appeared to run everything in the tent, according to radio instructions received from the Director, who was watching the proceedings from the toilet at the rear of the tent. He explained that they were just awaiting the arrival of "the talent". The talent being Mel and Sue with the Hollyberry. Once they had done their bit, we would then commence our "Signature" bake – the Swiss Roll.

The sides of the tent were open so we saw them approach, Mel and Sue followed by Mary Berry and Paul Hollywood. They stopped in the foyer of the tent while the makeup girls applied some last minute adjustment to the slap. Suitably preened the quartet approached their floor marks; once Brighty was happy with everything, they started to film. All said "good morning bakers" and Sue informed us that we were now required to start our Signature Bake. A quick good luck from the Hollyberry, a ready, steady, bake from Sue and we were off. From time to time, the Hollyberry would reappear with a camera crew and ask us what we were doing, how we were feeling and wish us good luck.

You will recall from Chapter Four that my proposed Signature bake for week one of the Bakeoff was to be a Black Forest "Swiss" Roll. This remained unchanged so I set off on the first step, making the sponge for the Swiss Roll. Once the sponge was in the oven, I started on the Morello Cherry jam. All went well with the Signature bake and Paul and Mary were suitably impressed with the result. I am not sure what happened to our bakes but once we had returned to the tent in the afternoon to start the Technical Challenge, there was no sign of them. Time keeping appeared to go all to pieces that first day; we had lunch at around 4 pm that is when I realised I should have eaten the Swiss Roll before leaving the tent.

Although we, the Bakers, had a trying time at some stages in the tent, I think the judges had a more difficult task, especially with picking the best and worst from the Technical Challenge. We all had to bake from the same recipe with identical ingredients. The resulting bakes were judged anonymously by Mary and Paul and ranked in order from twelfth to first. An extremely difficult task when they all looked identical. In our case with the cherry cake we had to bake, I think they had to search for something to criticise. Jordan managed to lose his cherries in the mix by chopping them up too finely so he was allocated twelfth place. My cake looked fine but was deemed "too dry" by Mary, which found me in eleventh position. Later I tasted the cake myself and found it was a bit dry, much like most of the others. I made this cake at home, with a similar result, it was again dry, this with a shorter oven time. I have concluded that this is a "dry" cake and have decided not to bake it again. In future, I will stick to my own cherry cake recipe, which is not as dry as Mary's one.

Our first day in the tent at an end, the taxis took us back to the hotel, arriving there at 9.00pm – a long day by anyone's standards. With the dining room closed we had a bar snack, I washed mine down with a couple of pints of Stella before retiring early in preparation for 6.20am on the Sunday morning when we would be baking our first "Showstopper".

Sunday morning 6.20am, we left the Mercure and arrived at Welford Park at 6.35 ready for the showstopper bake. Once again, we started the day with a cold bacon sandwich then it was off to the tent again to check the ingredients. On arrival in the tent, we all found it a touch hill-billy so on went the ovens – a quick way of warming up in the morning. My own showstopper was to be thirty-six almond and raspberry cakes with fresh cream so the ingredient check was fairly straightforward, just had to make sure I had plenty raspberries, to enable just the best looking ones to be used. The not so pretty ones would be used to make the jam. We headed back to the Green Room at around ten-thirty for another cup of coffee and returned to the tent once more to await the arrival of the "talent" and the commencement of the Showstopper Bake.

Assembled by our workstations we watched the Hollyberry arrive accompanied by Mel and Sue and after a few false starts, it was "Ready, Steady, Bake" and we were off on an intense three-hour journey. First task was to make the jam so I popped the raspberries in the processor then separated the juice from the seeds before boiling the juice with the sugar for ten minutes. Once the jam was made I set about making the cakes. This I accomplished in three separate batches of twelve each, allowing them all to cool before splitting them and filling with jam and cream. The tops were finished off with cream, raspberries, and a quick dusting of icing sugar. All complete within the allotted time......just!

We were then all ready to present our showstoppers to the judges and one at a time we had to walk forward and present our efforts for Paul and Mary's tasting and judging. I managed to get a positive response from both judges, although Paul did say it was a simple recipe but well executed. This "simple" comment was to be repeated each week, either on its own or with the addition of "plain". By week four I was thinking of bringing in a thesaurus, in the hope that they would be able to find some alternative words to describe my baking efforts.

At the end of the day, we all mounted our stools, which had been arranged in the tent in a large semi-circle. Paul, Mary, Mel & Sue then confronted us and announced the "star" baker. This well deserved accolade was awarded to Nancy. This announcement was followed by the breaking of the sad news that Claire was the one chosen to leave us. Very unfortunate we all thought, a very talented maker of cakes and a wonderful personality. However, it is a competition and someone has to go each week. It seems a difficult task for Paul and Mary but in comparison with some of the baking competitions I have had to judge since the Bakeoff, it is easy for them; they had to choose one loser each week whilst I have had to choose dozens of losers and one winner in numerous contests.

Sunday evening saw most of the bakers setting off for the railway station at Newbury and home; however, as the last flight north had left Heathrow and Gatwick, it was back to the hotel for a night on my own, a pint or two of Nelson and congratulating myself on not being the first baker to face elimination. The flight home had been arranged for the Monday morning as we had finished too late on the Sunday for me to catch the last flight. An uneventful journey back to Inverness saw me home by Monday lunchtime. I suppose I should have done a bit of practice for the following weeks baking but could not be bothered. Instead, I thought we would have a cheese soufflé for dinner, one of our favourites when you just cannot think of what you would like to eat. The recipe follows and this one always turns out perfectly, so have a look at this before we continue the rest of my adventures at Portknockie Primary School.

Cheese Souffle

Ingredients

100g mature cheddar cheese

4 large eggs separated

150ml milk

30g butter

30g flour (sauce flour or Italian 00 grade is best)

¼ teaspoon paprika

¼ teaspoon mustard powder

Salt and pepper

Method

Grease a one and a half pint soufflé dish and set your oven to 180 degrees fan.

Make a roux with the flour and butter and cook gently for three minutes.

Add the milk and simmer slowly for around four minutes.

Add the paprika, mustard, salt & pepper and leave to cool.

Whilst sauce is cooling grate the cheddar cheese and beat the egg yolks.

Once sauce is quite cool, add the cheese, stirring well and then add the egg yolks and set aside.

Whisk the egg whites until they are stiff then add a large spoonful of the whites to the sauce and mix in well before folding in the remainder of the whites. Be careful whilst folding in to ensure the air is retained in the mix. Pour the mix into the soufflé dish and take a knife round the edge at the top before baking at 180 degrees fan for 30 to 35 minutes or until it is as well done as you like it. Best eaten immediately.

CHAPTER TEN

Now Cooking At School

I had intended starting off this chapter with a bit about my year in Primary 5 but cannot recall anything good to say about that year, so I have decided to say nothing, leave Miss Bagwart alone and move on to the next year. In Primary Six, we had the good fortune to be taught by Mrs Archibald, a warm and wonderful human being who treated us with a very gentle hand, in direct contrast to the treatment meted out by some of the teachers we had so far experienced. As far as I can recall she never gave anyone the belt, in fact I am fairly certain she did not possess one. We had a very happy time in year six and by the time we moved into Mr Smith's class in year seven we had re-adjusted and were well prepared for anything Mr Smith could throw at us. He turned out to be almost as kind a soul as Mrs Archibald and I think we all enjoyed our time with him. He had an odd habit of sticking his tongue out the side of his mouth whilst writing on the blackboard, his left hand often in his pocket playing trouser billiards. Friday afternoons were the best, the boys weaved a scarf on a loom and the girls did some kind of sewing project, this was followed by a general knowledge quiz

At the end of year seven, they selected around two or three among the more academically talented pupils to go to Buckie High School and if one was really gifted and could cope with the classics, it was off in the other direction to Fordyce Academy. However, most of us were considered incapable of learning a foreign language and so carried on at Portknockie, in the Junior Secondary Department. In retrospect, I believe we had a very good education at Portknockie. Because a large number of the boys in Portknockie made the sea their career, either as fishermen or in the Merchant Navy, the curriculum at Portknockie fitted these careers perfectly. Those deciding against a sea-going life becoming shipwrights, carpenters or engineers at one of the three boat-building yards in Buckie. Apprenticeships in the building trades were also taken up by a few.

At Portknockie then we followed a maritime syllabus, being taught seamanship, nautical knowledge, chartwork, net making & mending, splicing rope and tying just about every knot, bend and hitch in the book, along with Rule of The Road at Sea and signalling.

The task of teaching the boys seamanship was carried out by the school janitor, Mr Peter Geddes, who had spent many years in the Merchant Navy and had worked as a fisherman. I don't think he had any formal teaching qualifications other than a devout passion for the subject, something we seldom encounter today. We were even taught how to use a bosun's chair from a height of 20+ feet. If Health & Safety had been around then they'd have had kittens! For the navigation side of things, Mr Moyes, the headmaster, gave us two charts to work with; the first one was the Southwestern Approaches to the English Channel, the second one a chart of the South China Sea. For the chartwork period, we had to lift long boards, like table-tops about twelve feet long to lie over the desks. This facilitated the spreading out of the charts. After plotting courses across the South China Sea and having read Ballantyne and Conrad, I decided quite early on in my teens that a seagoing career was the one for me and made my mind up to join the Merchant Navy once I left school.

It was usually the case that any boy going to sea on board a fishing boat would first be given the job of cook. Because of this, we were taught cooking and baking every Friday afternoon for the three years of our secondary education. This experience, I believe, helped kindle my interest in cooking and baking which I have retained throughout my life. I enjoyed Friday afternoons when we had the cooking class, of course being a class of boys you had to keep a constant watch on whatever you were cooking or baking. Learning to cook while trying to ensure no one threw a handful of salt or other undesired ingredient into your soup or stew was the norm. If the teacher was foolish enough to leave the room for a short period, that is when flour/rice/sugar/eggs or anything else to hand went flying across the room. It is a superfluous comment to say she only left us alone the once! After that, if she had to vacate the classroom at any time, she would call on the services of "Bull" the Science Master who would stand guard over us with a big stick until her return. Bull was also employed in a similar role to help our music teacher maintain order and to ensure we sang the correct words.

Being taught cooking and baking was excellent preparation for anyone's life; that, together with the other practical skills we learned at Portknockie, have stood us in good stead and helped many to cope with differing aspects of life, even if your job did not involve a hands-on role. In particular, at Portknockie we were taught woodwork and metalwork from age eleven. Our teacher was Mr Henderson, nickname Hindu. Whether the nickname was a corruption of his surname or not I am not sure as it may well have had a lot to do with his appearance, as he looked a touch far eastern, maybe Burmese. That he was a good teacher there is no doubt but he was a bit fussy regarding the exercises in woodwork and metalwork we had to carry out, it was either perfect or useless – nothing in between would satisfy. In our second year of woodwork, we were introduced to the wood lathe and as well as the metal lathe, we had a forge where we could pretend to be blacksmiths. All good fun you would think but at 3:45pm each woodwork day, we had to sweep the floor and account for every chisel, pencil, ruler etc. before being allowed home.

This 3-year apprenticeship in wood resulted in us going home either with a coffee table or in my case a bedside cabinet with a shelf and drawer, the beech wood being stained and finished in French polish. I still remember bringing it home and my Mam being unable to believe I had made it. It has lasted the years and I still have it. There a few scratches but the joints have remained firm, the animal glue must have done its stuff.

As I mentioned, some boys took home a coffee table. This was indeed something exotic in Portknockie, not a lot of people would ever have heard of a coffee table back then, in fact not a lot had tasted coffee as tea was the usual drink.

Most of our leisure time in Portknockie was spent outdoors, either swimming and fishing in the summer or building a hut or some other (usually unattainable) project. When I was thirteen we built a splendid hut within the ruins of an old building at the harbour. As they were then building some new houses in what would later be named Addison Street, we had a ready supply of timber. This was the time when I would be despatched to see my Grandad and ask to borrow a saw for a day or two. He usually got this back after two or three weeks then spent another few days resetting the saw and sharpening it. Nails we would buy from the local joiner, how this was done was easy; around four or five of went to see him in his workshop and ask to buy one pound or so of three-inch nails. Whilst he was getting them we'd be filling our pockets with anything that might come in handy, including whatever nails we could lay our hands on.

The completed hut was around twelve feet square with a sloping corrugated iron roof. Use was made of the old fireplace within the ruins of the building and a proper door fitted. Once complete we made great use of the hut during winter evenings with the fire lit and additional light from candles. Saturday night was the best; we would get hold of a bottle of beer and ten Strand cigarettes and with a pack of cards sit round the fire playing knockout whist pretending to be grownups. As far as growing up was concerned we all had a long way to go. We received no sex education at Portknockie School so imagination and second-hand stories were all we had to go on. As I said Saturday night was the best; one of the gang, Jake, who was a few years older than most of us, had got hold of a little red book at the Old Market whilst in Aberdeen one local holiday. It had cost him the princely sum of half-a-crown or twelve and a half pence in decimal currency. The book was called "The Red Light" and was a written description of everything to do with sex. Jake would read out loud a chapter every Saturday night. Some but not all of the secrets of the opposite sex were revealed to us before the book would be closed and we would be told there would be more next week! After a few choruses of "Four and twenty virgins" or some other ribald ditty, we would be off home, Mam asking what you had been doing. Only to be told "nothing", the usual answer to every question, either that or "It wisnae me!"

We enjoyed the winter nights in our hut but come the springtime we had decided to build a raft. The hut was dismantled for this purpose and construction commenced – back to Granda for the saw and a warning not to saw through any nails with it. Talking of nails, it was also back to the joiner again for more. Construction of the raft continued through spring and into summertime. The shape of our raft resembled an oversized sentry box. As it was made entirely of wood we were faced with a problem, we had to waterproof the joints. This, we decided would require pitch and in some quantity. Fortunately, Fatty had a pal at Buckie High School; yes, he was so clever they sent him there in a bus every day from Portknockie. Fatty's pal lived near one of the boatyards in Buckie and he knew where the pitch boiler was located. Three of us set off one night in the bus for Buckie and met Fatty's pal who led us through a gap in the fence into the boatyard and thence to the pitch boiler. We loaded three sacks with what we thought was sufficient pitch for the job and set off for the bus stop, with frequent stops, as the sacks were very heavy. The bus arrived and the driver helped us load the sacks into the boot of the bus. He was curious as to what we were carrying in the sacks so we just told him it stones off the beach for my Granny's rockery.

The next problem we encountered was how to melt the pitch we had purloined. The solution was found when I remembered about the old washhouse boiler we had at home. This was located in what was known as the "Eek-Tee" – a long corrugated iron roofed building stuck on to the side of Summerton. This was a wood-fired boiler but with a large cast iron tub above the fire box. We lifted this out and carried it down to our "boat-yard" where, after mounting it on some large boulders, we were ready to light a fire and melt the pitch. The tub looked very much like a smaller version of the cartoon pots they used in Africa to boil missionaries. Once we had melted the pitch, we gave all the joints in the raft a good coating of pitch inside and out. This did not happen of course without a few burnt fingers!

All was then ready for us to set a launch date but we were in for a huge disappointment; the local bobby had been watching what we had been up to all summer. He had let us carry on with the raft building, if we were busy with something he probably thought we would be kept out of trouble for a while. The bobby had gone round all our parents letting them know what we were up to and advising them of the imminent launch. Our parents could foresee disaster if we managed to launch the raft and asked the bobby to tell us we were not allowed to launch the raft and would have to break it up. All that work for nothing!

What happened next you could not make up; Jeemsie Soutar's dog died and he was going to bury him so we had the brilliant idea of giving Patch (the dog) a Viking funeral. So it was that one moonlit evening in August, we launched the raft on an outgoing tide, and carefully placed Patch inside. We then set light to a bundle of paraffin soaked rags in the raft and pushed it out to sea. With all that pitch on board you can imagine the fire. As the tide receded and the sun sank below the horizon, we watched Patch on his way to Valhalla. He sailed away until midnight when the fire dimmed and we think the raft sank. No hut and no raft but school was due to recommence in a week's time. Now fourteen this was to be my last year.

Sex education aside we did have a splendid learning experience at Portknockie, it was entirely relevant to life but unfortunately such learning would not be so appropriate today. Where once there were three boat-building yards in Buckie, today they are all gone. In 1957, the three yards in Buckie built 21 fishing boats, all in the region of 70 ft. The British Merchant Navy was the biggest in the World. Companies like the Bank Line of Glasgow had over seventy ships plying trade routes covering the four corners of the globe. The question in your mind on leaving Portknockie School at fifteen was not; "Am I going to get a job?" it was more "What job will I do? There was plenty work available and I do not believe anyone found any difficulty in getting employment. Today, with the decline in the fishing, the entire area is almost completely dependent on the oil industry for employment, unfortunately now even its coat is on a shoogly peg.

My own goal remained unchanged at fifteen, I was going to join the Merchant Navy; initially I had intended to join as a deck apprentice and applied to the Robert Gordon School of Navigation in Aberdeen, hoping to be accepted for the one-year pre-apprenticeship course they ran there. Having had the necessary grounding at Portknockie I was already halfway toward taking the examination for Second Mate Foreign Going, all I needed was a bit more study, particularly on ship stability and cargo loading, plus of course a few years sea-time. However, a friend of the family, himself a captain in the MN had said to my Mam that it was quite a difficult course I was setting myself. He said you had to be very clever to pass all the examinations required. This fact, coupled with some information gained from a cousin of my father's, resulted in my being sent to the Wireless College in Aberdeen to do the 18 month to 2 year course for Radio Officer MN. I then took up residence at number 252 Holburn Street, Aberdeen – just opposite the (old) Holburn Bar, under the watchful eye of Mrs Kirk the landlady. Looking back, I realise now that it would have been far easier to have gone to sea as a deck apprentice, most of the ones I met at sea had no more maritime knowledge than myself and the radio & telecommunications course was very difficult, requiring a lot of study. There was a sixty per cent dropout rate but I passed the necessary exams in the end (I failed the practical at the first attempt) and became fully qualified as Radio Officer just before I was seventeen, all ready for the far side of the World.

In the winter months, if we have just a plate of soup and bread for lunch, we sometimes treat ourselves to oven cooked rice pudding or as we knew it in the Merchant Navy, "Chinese Wedding Cake". What follows is a simple recipe and serves two people with a decent helping.

Chinese Wedding Cake

Ingredients

50g pudding rice (the round grain type, similar in shape to Arboria rice)

1 x 170ml can evaporated milk

250ml whole milk or semi-skimmed if you prefer

50g granulated sugar

25g butter

A little grated nutmeg

Method

Set your oven to 160 degrees C or 150 degrees C fan.

In a medium sized casserole dish, add the rice, evaporated milk, whole milk and sugar and stir a little. Dot the surface with wee bits of butter and sprinkle with the nutmeg. Do not cover and place on the middle shelf of the oven for around 90 minutes. Check after one hour, you want to end up with a nice brown skin on top and a creamy consistency so don't let it dry out too much.

Serve with a tablespoon of raspberry jam or some fruit if you prefer.

Warning, this only serves two people and there will be none left.

CHAPTER ELEVEN

The Bakeoff Week Two – Biscuits

Friday 2nd of May arrived and I set off once more for Inverness Airport to board the flight for Gatwick, eventually making my way to Newbury where I met the other ten bakers at Nandos, a restaurant chain where they sold dead hens for a quick twelve quids worth of beer and chicken. After this magnificent repast, the taxis arrived and took us back to Percy's old home and a night's kip prior to getting our teeth into the second Bakeoff week, the Biscuit Week.

Out of bed before six; it is funny once you retire, how you forget there are two six o'clocks! Once again, no breakfast at the hotel, so we assisted Luis with all his kit and boarded the taxis for the short drive to the tent, with the vain hope in our hearts that the bacon sandwiches would be a bit warmer than last week. Unfortunately, breakfast was again a little less than inspiring but at least I had my biscuits to look forward to. We sat around in the green room, drinking coffee and chatting until nine-thirty; then we were summoned by Murray who led us into the tent, where we were instructed to check the ingredients prepared for us for the Signature Bake. That is in fact one of the enjoyable aspects of baking in the tent, the Home Economics people place all the ingredients for your bake on your bench for you. Even more appreciated was the fact that someone else washed up all the dishes. For series five, we had the services of a lady who washed up all our bowls, beaters and baking trays by hand. There was no mechanical dishwasher as this would have made too much noise in the tent and risked upsetting the soundmen - they had enough problems already with aircraft flying overhead. We were buzzed, on one occasion at least, by Murray's dad, who as a helicopter test pilot regularly flew over the area.

Ingredients all present and correct we strolled back to the green room, more coffee and maybe a jellybean or two if you got there before Luis. Finally, we were called into the tent at around 11 am and stood at attention by our benches, once more awaiting the arrival of the talent. They appeared along with the make-up team and after a quick good morning from the Hollyberry, Mel and Sue gave us the ready, steady, bake and we were off.

Three dozen biscuits and an hour and a half to produce them. My ingredients were relatively straightforward and I had plenty time to rub in the fats to the flour by hand. I prepared the biscuits in batches of 18 and had both batches baked within 35 minutes, plenty of time to cool and display my biscuits for the judging. Mary and Paul were very impressed with the finished article and Paul went as far as to shake my hand in congratulating me on a task well executed. One of the senior producers came up to me later and said I had done well to get the handshake as he (Paul) seldom afforded any contestant such an accolade.

Back to the green room for lunch, more hanging around, and of course more coffee before returning to the tent in the afternoon to make a start on the Technical Challenge. This turned out to be something I had heard of but never eaten – Florentines. The recipe was very straightforward and there appeared to be little difference between our individual biscuits. The only one standing out a bit being Enwezor, he cut his to shape after baking – a mistake according to Mary. My own were not in last position although they were not placed too highly up the ladder, this despite the fact that they were all almost identical with little to choose between them all. This is what happens with the technical judging, unless there are any obvious disasters, the selection of best to worst can be quite arbitrary. However, that was the technical over with, just the 3D biscuit display to do on the Sunday. Meantime back to the hotel for a quick Nelson and a chat with the rest of the gang before ordering a snack and off to bed.

On with the show then on this the Showstopper Day. We spent the usual first hour or so sitting in the Green Room drinking coffee before being ushered into the tent to check that all our ingredients were present and correct. This task completed we retired once more to the Green Room before our return to the tent around 11 am, just in time to greet the judges and jesters before being once more given the "Ready Steady Bake". I reacted to this in my usual way – staring into space for a minute or so before consulting my recipe and bashing on with the biscuit making. I made all the bits for the boats and sails first before assembling using boiling sugar as the glue – very effective but just had to watch the fingers!. This was followed by making the Italian meringue with blue food colouring for the sea. I also made a couple of herring baskets using choux pastry along with their contents of fish-shaped biscuits coloured silver. The whole was then assembled with the four and a half hour allotted time, I decided against the light-house I had planned to include in the display after one of the producers made the comment that it was a bit risque in appearance.

All done, we marched up to the judges individually, displaying the day's work. Because you believe in what you have just done, you always feel a bit deflated with even the slightest criticism of your efforts. Today was no exception; again, I was told that my 3D display was a bit plain, despite the fact that I had spent some time in decorating a pair of "Zulu" shields. I was particularly proud of the choux pastry baskets I had made, but these were rejected out of hand as "not being made of biscuit". I thought this an unfair remark bearing in mind the wide range of "baking" that had been used in most of the other contestants' displays. There is no order given from best to worst in the Showstopper, however, I would say that the George and Dragon by Luis was phenomenal, very well planned, skilfully executed and I do believe Luis got the "handshake" from Paul. Richard also received a great deal of praise for his Pirates Island display but Enwezor came in for a bit of stick from Mary for using "shop-bought" fondant and marzipan – he got one of Mary's looks. My own favourite was Jordan's display even though he had "lost" two bits – a building and an aeroplane – but later found them at the side of his bench. Once the judging was over with we had to have various shots filmed of our efforts, this seemed to take forever when all we wanted was to get out of the tent. Eventually we were dismissed and set off for a late lunch before returning to the tent, there to find out which one of us would be getting their marching orders that day.

I think it was around 4pm when we were all summoned to the tent. We sat on our stools – arranged in a semi-circle facing the Hollyberry, Mel & Sue. Sue then announced the "Star" baker – Luis, yes, very well deserved. Then Mel had the difficult task of telling Enwezor that it was goodbye, adios, auf viedersehn, tata. I think he kind of knew the game was up once he'd had the "look" from Mary re the "shop-bought" fondant, he smiled anyway and everyone gave him a hug, including Mary and Paul. The other bakers then headed for Newbury railway station for their journey home. Luis got in his car and headed for Manchester and once more it was too late for me to catch the last flight from Gatwick, so back to Shelley's Shack for another night before my flight on Monday morning.

I phoned Iris and told her I had escaped dismissal for another week, although I think it was a near thing between Enwezor and me, that is according to one of the producers anyway, but I think they used to say that to everyone. To celebrate my second week of the Bakeoff I had a coupla pints of Stella Artois and a snack meal in the hotel bar. Being very tired, I slept like a log until getting up at 7am in time for my taxi to Newbury Station and on to Gatwick. Having had no breakfast for three days I had the Full Monty at Jamie Oliver's restaurant at Gatwick whilst waiting for my flight. The breakfast was superb and in my mind well worth the tenner it cost me!

The flight to Inverness had me back home and putting my feet up by lunchtime and left me thinking about maybe a bit of practice for the third week of the Bakeoff – Bread Week. Before that, I would like to tell you about my leaving school and going off to the Wireless College in Aberdeen. First, though, you might like to have a look at my recipe for my Chicken, Tarragon & Mushroom pie, finished in a rough puff pastry case. This is the very recipe I used for the pie I brought to London for the Extra Slice programme, it was tasted by none other than Michel Roux jnr and he pronounced it superb with a nice flavour of tarragon. A fantastic compliment from a Michelin Star Chef.

Chicken Tarragon and Mushroom Pie

Pastry

200g plain flour

½ tsp salt

65g butterfly

65g lard

Few tbsps. Chilled water

The Filling

2 chicken breasts

100g shitake or chesnut mushrooms

3 tsp fresh tarragon or 2 tsp dried

1 shallot or small onion

25g butter

25g flour

Around 10 fl ozs milk warmed

Method

First make the rough puff pastry.

Sift the flour and salt into a mixing bowl.

Cut the butter and lard into cubes of around 3 to 5mm square and add to the flour, mixing well with a knife. Do not rub in the fat but leave in lumps.

Bring together with chilled water to form a dough and roll out to around 30cm x 10cm and fold the bottom third up and the top third down on top, make a quarter turn and repeat a further twice before placing in the refrigerator to chill.

Chop the onion or shallot and place in a small frying pan with the mushrooms and a little oil and fry until onion is soft and translucent, set aside to cool.

Place the chicken breasts in a small casserole with 20g butter, pinch salt & pepper and one tea-spoon tarragon, cover and bake at 170 degs C for 25 mins then remove from oven and allow to cool before shredding by hand. Add the 25g butter and 25g flour to a small saucepan and mix together and cook for 2 to 3 minutes then add the milk slowly, stirring until a nice reasonably thick sauce is made. Add the chicken to the sauce along with the onion and mushroom, season with salt and pepper and the tarragon, mixing well.

Divide the chilled pastry in two, using one part to roll out very thinly and line the base and sides of a suitable pie dish or 23cm tart tin. Add the chicken, mushroom and sauce mixture before rolling out the other half of the pastry and covering the pie. Finish off the top with decoration from the cuttings, glaze with beaten egg and sprinkle a little oregano, black pepper & sea salt on top. Bake at 200 degrees C for 30 minutes then reduce heat to 180 degrees C for a further 20 minutes.

CHAPTER TWELVE

To Aberdeen Wireless College

The tender age of fifteen years and two months saw me depart Portknockie, taking the two hour train journey to Aberdeen and ultimately to the lodging house of Mrs Kirk at 252 Holburn Street. This was to be home for the next two years. I recall being very apprehensive about living away from home, the main concern being the food; other than a few days at my Grannies and the two weeks in hospital when I was six, I'd always been fed on the food my mother prepared. I had no idea what I was in for with Mrs Kirk doing the cooking; she was English, from Oldham, and had met Mr Kirk, an Aberdonian, during the war. Mrs Kirk had been a bus conductress and Mr Kirk was in the British Army. Not sure what he was doing in Oldham, I do not think there were many Germans there. Mr Kirk did not have a job due to health reasons; instead, he helped run the lodging house. It must have been quite hard work for both of them as they had two sons and sixteen lodgers to take care of. We got full board for seven days at a cost of £3-10/- and that included breakfast, lunch, tea and a cup of tea and one sandwich (small) at 9pm. We slept three to a bedroom and each of us had our own bed; Mr Kirk said he would never have two men sharing a bed as he had seen enough of that carry-on in the army!

Toilet facilities were inadequate to say the least; we had one bathroom for twenty people, so mornings were always a rush. However, two or three of the bedrooms had a large jug of hot water and a basin delivered each morning, which did take the pressure off the bathroom. We seldom made use of the bath at 252; instead, we used to walk toward Holburn Junction and into the Bon Accord baths where one could soak in a huge bath for the princely sum of one shilling. Each bath had its own private cubicle, the only snag being the fact that the hot and cold taps were located outside the cubicle. This would have meant having to get out of the bath to add more hot or cold water. However, there was a woman on duty outside - I think her main task was cleaning etc. – and she was in charge of the taps. So you would hear the shouts go up every few minutes – "Mair caul in number echt", or "Mair hait in number twa". Being deep and warm there was always a reluctance to get out of the bath but the water controller also kept note of your time, I think it was around twenty minutes you were allowed before getting the shout "Number five, get oot!

 There were sixteen of us in digs at 252, made up of six students at Aberdeen Wireless College, including yours truly, five students of architecture, one civil servant, two medical students, a motorcycle mechanic and Corporal Pike of the Royal Signals who was in charge of the Territorial Army Depot at Fonthill just across the way from the digs. Fortunately, the different groups appeared at different times in the mornings with the architecture students usually appearing last. They seemed to spend most nights at the Student Union until the last two weeks of term when they spent most of the time and usually into the small hours of the morning drawing pictures of houses, in a desperate effort to catch up. Some of them never did. The medical students studied all the time, they must have had a shed-load of stuff to memorise, and one of them had a skeleton under his bed – a real one! We at the Wireless College had a fair bit of studying to do as well and at colder times (most of the year) we would relocate in the evenings to the Reference Library at the end of Union Terrace where it was nice and warm and do our studying there. The alternative was to study in our rooms at 252; however, there was no heating apart from a one-bar fire, which only came to life if someone could be persuaded to insert a shilling in the meter. That was something I never reverted to, I did get some pocket money, adequate perhaps but not to be squandered on an electricity meter. My father paid the digs for me and my mother gave me £1 each week for pocket money. I used to have a weekend at home every two or three weeks when my mother would send me a £1 for the train fare. This was where I made a bit of extra pocket money. The adult fare was around 17/6d but I would buy a half fare, weekend return to Inverurie and go all the way to Portknockie. No one checked the tickets and I was usually a good fifteen bob better off. That was seventy-five pence in today's money, not a lot you might think but remember in those days a pint was less than 10p and ten cigarettes around 12p.

Bearing in mind the cost of a full week's board and lodging, the food was not too bad, perhaps just not enough of it but nobody starved. The mince was a touch more watery than you would get at home and two fish fingers for tea did little to curb a youthful appetite. The highlight of

Mrs Kirk's lodgings was the coffee in the morning. Coming from Portknockie I had not drunk much coffee and so it was something to behold when I first saw the coffee percolator. This was a huge chrome affair with the appearance of a Russian Samovar. It had a glass bubble on top through which you could see the coffee percolating. The percolator was located on a small table on its own where the day's mail was also laid out and you could serve yourself with a nice cupful by turning a tap at the bottom. To this day, I have not tasted coffee as good as the stuff Mrs Kirk gave us; I only wish I had found out the name or blend. I have always taken my coffee black and so the taste meant more to me than if I had taken milk in it. In addition to the coffee, we got toast and whatever was being dished up that day; a poached egg, beans on toast, scrambled egg and on Sundays, bacon, egg and a tattie scone. Sundays we always got a lie-in, as breakfast was not served until 9am.

Aberdeen Wireless College was located at No.7 Albyn Terrace opposite the SAI Offices – Scottish Agricultural Industries - although we were always told it was the Scottish Artificial Insemination Building, where young lassies milked the bulls for sperm. There was a large intake of new students in August that year; I think we had around twenty-five new starts. They were a very mixed bunch, ranging in age from seventeen to some in their late twenties. A mix of university dropouts, older men looking for a career change, failed apprentices and a number of ex forces personnel. The syllabus did present quite a challenge but I managed to keep pace with the rest without too much trouble.

We would leave the digs in Holburn Street at around 8:45 for the ten-minute walk to Albyn terrace and the College. The course was quite intense, nine to five each day with only a three week summer break. The day was divided into the practical part, including morse code practice and telecommunications regulations. The other half being devoted to electricity and magnetism, radiocommunication principles and general electronic theory. We had a ten-minute break in the morning and the afternoon with a one-hour lunch break, which saw us heading back to 252 to savour Mrs Kirk's lunchtime offering. Mr Kirk grew brussels sprouts in the garden and we were quite often served soup containing sprouts, you could smell it from the other end of Nellfield Place! Evenings were spent studying or more likely playing cards, games like Mizaire and Hearts being very popular.

119

May 1963 saw myself and Jeemsie Slater, a fellow student, planning a continental Youth Hostelling trip. Our imaginations had been fired by tales from another, older student George Howitt who had served in the RAF in Germany. We reckoned on being able to hitchhike at least as far as Germany. Later a fourth student, Raymond Melvin was recruited to the gang and we set about preparing for the adventure to take place during the summer break. First of all a passport was obtained, I already had my SYHA Membership card, a rucksack, a decent pair of walking boots and a waterproof anorak. All I required then was some money. Somehow I managed to convince my mother to let me have £25 from my savings which I converted into travellers cheques, convinced that was enough to finance a three week trip. £25 was indeed a large sum of money for a sixteen year old in 1963 and in those days, we were getting over twelve German Marks to the pound and a night in the Jugendherberge in Germany cost two marks fifty pfennigs. All ready then we planned to set off on the 29th June.

I already had a pair of walking boots - the ones with commando soles, £3-5/- from Millets – but needed something else for my feet in the warm weather. I paid a visit to Taylors Art Salon in Schoolhill and bought a pair of DIY moccasins, the ones you had to stitch up yourself with leather thongs. Can't really remember how much they cost me but I think it was around 17/6d, anyhow they looked good and did the job. So nine o'clock in the morning of the 29th saw us make our way to the Bridge of Dee before splitting up, we thought it would be much easier to get lifts if we were singles. In any case I did not fancy accompanying Jeemsie on lifts, the month previous we were on a weekend climb of Lochnagar and had hitchhiked back to Aberdeen on the Sunday. We got a good lift from Ballater from a nice lady who said she was going all the way to Aberdeen – perfect. Unfortunately, Jeemsie had had a large tin of beans and two eggs for breakfast with the inevitable result, so the lady pulled up in Aboyne saying she had to visit someone there. We watched as she departed – on the road to Aberdeen!

We split up at the Bridge of Dee planning to meet up again at the Youth Hostel in Dover two days later. I got a lift quite quickly in a lorry heading for Newcastle then a further two lifts to somewhere south of Scotch Corner. I was then picked up by a chap from London and his wife; they were driving an A35. He very kindly took me all the way to London and dropped me off at the British Drivers Club in Tooley Street, a hostel for lorry drivers. He advised me to put any cash and valuables below my pillow as I slept. I thanked this kind family and checked in at the hostel. A bed in a room with four beds was 8/- whilst one in a room with eight beds was 4/-. I opted for the more expensive room and slept like a log, waking up at seven in the morning and relieved to find my wallet and passport still below the pillow.

I made my way to the London Underground, London Bridge Station and boarded a train for Victoria where I bought a ticket for Gillingham, Kent, as I thought that was clear of London and on the way to Dover and I would get a lift from there without too much trouble. It took me a while to get to Dover but I eventually arrived there by late afternoon when I checked in at the Youth Hostel and awaited the arrival of the other heroes. They eventually arrived in dribs and drabs and we found ourselves billeted in what they called the "Seagull's Nest" on the sixth floor of the hostel, overlooking the Straits of Dover.

Around eight in the evening we set off for the town, I have no recollection of the pubs we visited but do remember drinking rather a lot of something called "Brown & Mild" as recommended by Howitt; he'd been here before and thought that stuff was drinkable and good value. It must have been OK as I think I had six or seven pints – not bad for a sixteen year old. As I recall no one asked our age, perhaps we looked older than our years, which is certainly the case nowadays! Having a great night out in Dover meant we missed the ten o'clock curfew at the hostel and we had to knock on the door to get the warden to open up, he did not seem to be very happy as we made our inebriated way to the sixth floor. There were around twenty hostellers sleeping on the sixth floor, and a good mix of nationalities, none of whom appreciated our late arrival. A wee bit of a fracas ensued with some pillows and stuff being thrown out of the window. Peace was restored by the warden's arrival, and after he had threatened to confiscate our membership cards, we went to bed and fell asleep immediately. Eight in the morning saw us trying to rustle up some breakfast, I won't forget Melvin's face as he sat with head in hands and the sweat running off him – he had finished off the evening with some whisky and he was feeling very sorry for himself.

Later that day we made our way to the ferry terminal to board the midday ferry for Belgium. As we were planning going through Germany we thought that the best route was via Ostende, even if the fare was a bit more expensive at four pounds return. After boarding the ferry, we started planning our route for the next three weeks or so. As Liege in Belgium was within striking distance at 130 miles, we decided to make that our first destination. Liege had a youth hostel so we decided to split up again on arrival at Ostende and meet in the evening at the hostel in Liege. On arrival and before setting off to hitch to Liege we had a meal at a seafront café, fried mussels and chips, which was the first time I'd had them in batter and I think the last. After the meal and our first glass of Belgian beer, we set off on the road to Liege and the Youth Hostel where we all met up and spent the night before heading for Koblenz the next day.

Of all the hostels or Jugendherberge I visited on the continent, I found the one at Koblenz the most memorable. It was located in the Ehrenbreitstein Fortress overlooking the Deutsches Eck at the confluence of the Moselle and Rhine Rivers, a magnificent view although quite an uphill hike to get there. We are planning a trip to Germany this summer and hope to revisit Koblenz, including the Ehrenbreitstein Fortress; however, this time we can take the new cable car, which runs from the Deutsches Eck to near the fortress entrance. I think it costs around ten euro for the return trip but that will save the old legs a bit. You never know we might just walk up and spend the ten euro on beer, which seems a more sensible idea. The night I spent in the Ehrenbreitstein Fortress at Koblenz, I experienced the most magnificent thunderstorm I have ever lived through. The dormitory windows were all open to the night air and the resounding cracks of thunder and brilliant flashes of lightning were something to behold. It was not unlike a scene from a Dracula or Frankenstein movie, very spectacular and you could smell the ozone.

The next day I visited a fruit market on the opposite bank of the Rhine and bought a kilo bag of cherries. That is another outstanding memory, sitting on the banks of the river, spitting cherry stones into the Rhine. Next stop was to be the Hostel at Mainz but first a long walk to the outskirts of Koblenz. Mainz was followed by Mannheim then over the border to Switzerland, stopping at Basle then Zurich. I passed quickly through Lichtenstein, experiencing the heaviest rain I'd ever come across, fortunately I was able to shelter in a roadside tavern where I lunched on kartoffel salad, knackwurst & rye bread, washed down with a nice bottle of pils. Over another border to Austria and a night in Innsbruck before meeting up with the rest of the gang in Salzburg. We split up again and that was the last I saw of them until I resumed college in August when we all had a few tales to tell.

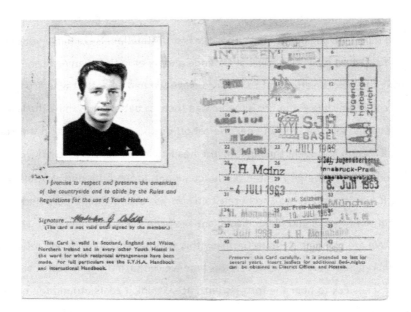

My Youth Hostel membership Card 1963

Leaving Salzburg behind, I set off for Munich and another jugendeherberger, some more potato salad and sausage before making a return visit to Mannheim. I had not really intended making a second visit to Mannheim but the first lift I got was from a telephone engineer – Bundes something or other – and he was going all the way to Mannheim. Likewise, when I left Mannheim, I got a lift to Koblenz, which quite pleased me, as I had been very impressed with the hostel and its location. In fact, I enjoyed it so much that I spent two nights there. I was really getting into the German hostel food by now and of course, it was cheap – just half a crown (12-1/2p in new money) got you sausage, potato salad and bread plus a cup of ersatz coffee. I think that repast was the German equivalent of pie, beans & chips. I was getting on very well with the Germans I thought; of course, I did remember not to mention "zee var". It was remarkable to consider the fact that twenty years earlier, I would have been shot as a spy!

I spent another two days at Koblenz before deciding that it was time I headed for Ostende and ultimately home. I was on my way again on the 13th of July, this time going via Aachen on the German/Belgian border. I was unable to make Aachen in a single day as lifts were not easy and the Polizei arrested me when they caught me hitching a lift on the Autobahn approach road. They took me to the police station and lectured me on "Autostop autobahn ist verboten!", or words to that effect. They let me go after a few hours and I spent the night in a roadside barn on the way to Aachen. The Aachen jugendherberger turned out to be just as comfortable a hostel as Koblenz, so I stayed there two nights before heading for Ostende and the ferry. It was at the hostel that I met some people from Manchester on their way to Bavaria for a holiday. I do not remember all their names, only one in particular, Michael Hall, who used to send me a Christmas card every year but I think he gave up after a few years when he was not getting one in return.

I managed to reach Ostend and boarded the night ferry for Dover, docking early in the morning of the 17th July. I had in my pocket 2/6d, which is 12-1/2p in today's cash. I bought myself a bottle of lemonade and a pie hoping that would last until I got home. The pie was gone by London, likewise the lemonade by Stevenage. Ten o'clock that evening found me in Scottish border country, in Coldstream. I bedded down in a bus shelter there using my moccasins as a pillow, getting a lift to Perth first thing in the morning. It was not until I arrived in Perth that I discovered I had left the moccasins behind in Coldstream. The lorry driver who had given me the lift from Coldstream was stopping at Perth so I made my way to the transport café there. I had no cash but offered to do some washing up or cleaning tables in return for food. I was in luck as they were very busy that day and so I spent a couple of hours in the kitchen washing dishes, also helped clearing tables. My reward was pie, beans and chips, bread & butter & a mug of tea. More importantly I'd spoken to a lorry driver who has was on his way north and he said I could have a lift all the way to Aberdeen, he said he was tired and thought I could help keep him awake. Unfortunately, I fell asleep just after leaving Dundee; "Fat lot of good you were!" he said when he let me off in Anderson Drive Aberdeen.

From Anderson Drive, I made my way to the lodging house at 252 and had a short conversation with Mrs Kirk to let her know I would be back on board the following week to re-commence studies at the Wireless College. After she gave me a sharp tonguing for not letting my mother know where I was (Mam had been on the phone), I was on my way hitching back to Portknockie. I actually had let my mother know where I was by sending a postcard on two occasions; unfortunately, I had taken the cheaper postage option and sent them by surface mail and I arrived home before the postcards. That reminds me of the World Cup in Argentina 1978, there was a great deal of hype regarding Scotland's chances and Ally's Tartan Army. Tommy Docherty summed this up very well with his famous quote "They'll be home before the postcards". To be fair Scotland did very well, beating The Netherlands and just narrowly missing qualifying for the next round.

For years now, I have experimented with various recipes for scones and it was not until I tried Paul Hollywood's recipe for scones using strong flour, that I realised I had found the perfect scone recipe. The recipe, which follows, is for Cheese Scones but is based upon Paul's strong flour recipe. I had never tasted a cheese scone until quite recently when my daughter Louise bought me one while we were at Christies in Fochabers for afternoon tea. I enjoyed it so much I decided to make my own, this recipe is the result. Using a 6cm cutter should yield around ten scones if you roll out to around 12mm thick

Cheese Scones

Ingredients

250g strong flour

2-1/2 tsp baking powder

½ tsp mustard powder

½ tsp salt

Pinch smoked paprika

130g grated cheese - mixed if you like, I used Cheddar, Havarti & Parmesan but try with any cheese, I just happened to have these three in the fridge today.

40g butter

1 large egg

130ml milk

Method

Set your oven to 220 degs C non-fan. I find scones have more chance of an even rising with a non-fan setting, at least with my own oven, a Neff slide and hide…..I bought one after the Bakeoff, but really should have got it before. A bit like my Kitchen Aid, that was only purchased after the first week of the Bakeoff, prior to that I didn't own a stand mixer.

Add to a large bowl, the flour, baking powder, mustard powder, salt, and paprika. Using a second bowl sift all these dry ingredients five times. Rub in the 40g butter, you could use a processor but it is hardly worth it for such a small quantity. Add the 130g of grated cheese and mix well.

Add the egg to 100ml of the milk and beat well. Keep the 30ml milk aside as you may or may not need it all to finish your scones. Make a well in the dry ingredients and add the egg/milk mix and blend together using the 30ml milk if necessary to make a very soft sticky dough. Using a good dusting of flour on your work surface transfer the dough and massage it gently until smooth, do not overmix and do not knead. Roll out to 12mm thick and relax the dough before cutting out your scones.

Using a 6cm cutter dipped in flour cut the scones out and place on baking parchment on a baking tray, 2cm apart. Do not twist the cutter and be sure to dip cutter in flour before each cut. Brush excess flour from the tops and glaze the tops only using a beaten egg. If you are short of eggs or would like to economise, you could always reserve a teaspoon of beaten egg from your mix, add some milk, and use this for your glaze.

Allow the scones to rest for fifteen minutes, this will give the rising agent time to work, before placing on the top shelf of the oven for twelve minutes or until nicely browned on top. Once baked allow to cool before eating. These are excellent with a plate of tomato or French Onion soup. They freeze very well and are just like fresh ones if placed in the microwave for fifteen seconds on the defrost setting.

I have recently seen a tip from Mr Hollywood. After cutting out your scones place them on the baking tray and keep in the refrigerator for one hour. Before popping in the oven, flip the scones over, glaze with beaten egg and bake as usual. I have tried this on several occasions and it does appear to give a uniform rise to the scones.

CHAPTER THIRTEEN

Week Three of The Bakeoff - Bread

Week three of the Bakeoff kicked off with us meeting in the foyer of the Hotel Mercure Elcot Park before boarding a couple of taxis bound for the culinary delights of the Hoggit and Hoof in nearby Newbury. The usual twelve pounds, per diem, was issued and we had a very pleasant evening with the meal being quite enjoyable, then it was back to the Mercure. Following a few hours sleep, we once more left the hotel in what felt like the middle of the night, arriving at the tent at six-forty am. A bacon roll and lots of coffee helped us pass the time until we were summoned to the tent to check over all our ingredients for the Signature Bake. Week Three was Bread Week, the Signature Bake being one dozen rye bread rolls. The ingredients all checked, we toddled back to the Green Room to do some more waiting and coffee drinking. Another hour or so wasted you would think but it gave the bakers time to apply lipstick and check the hair, and that was just the men.

At ten thirty, we were back in the tent, awaiting the arrival of the talent – that was four hours after we had arrived at Welford Park. They duly arrived and were once more subject to some last minute titillation from the makeup squad. Paul H had his hair touched up; they kept the jelly from the tops of pork pies especially for this purpose. Once they had said their good mornings, Sue asked us to start the proceedings with twelve rye bread rolls. No one appeared to have any problems with this task, the only rolls that could be described as truly outstanding were the ones baked by Luis. He made crescent shaped ones with two different colours of dough; these earned Luis the 'handshake' from Paul and a sincere well done from everybody else. The other rolls were very similar; date & walnut, wildebeest & banana, knotweed & neep etc., most of them having two items of flavouring including my own caraway seed and sultana ones. However, Paul said – once more – that they were very simple. In fact, they were no simpler than anyone else's. It really needed to be asked, what was the difference in simplicity between date & walnut and caraway seed & sultana. I rest my case. Paul also stated that my rolls tasted bland, not surprising since he had just had a mouthful of Chetna's chutney which was packed with chillies and very spicy. To be honest, he probably would not have been able to taste anything for a fortnight – bland?.

We all enjoyed our lunch that day and had quite a discussion as to what the "Technical Bake" would be in the afternoon. As it was Bread Week, we knew it would be one of Paul's recipes. All of us were all pretty well relaxed by this time, knowing that whatever it was, the yeast was going to do most of the work. That is the best thing about bread week; you do spend a lot of time waiting for dough to prove. Once we had re-assembled at our benches, Sue told us of the afternoon's assignment; Mary and Paul advised us to be "patient" with the task ahead and disappeared for their afternoon nap. The announcement was then made – "Ciabatta" and we had three hours to complete four ciabatta loaves. Fortunately for me, I had made ciabatta loaves at home the previous week. I expected to do well with this one and I was not far wrong, being placed fourth out of ten. I felt I could just as easily have been placed first, but heigh-ho.

The first day of the third week over with, we returned to the hotel, hoping for a drink and a bar snack/meal. Unfortunately the main bar lounge on the ground floor was closed for refurbishment so we had to use the downstairs bar. Not a problem, we thought; however when we tried to order food we were informed that we could not have food there due to health and safety regulations – they were not permitted to carry food downstairs. After we had a drink or two we repaired to Iain's room and a couple of the guys went ashore to get an Indian carryout from Newbury. Once we had the carryout, we called room service for some forks and plates. One of the flunkeys arrived and seemed to take a dim view of our efforts to feed ourselves. We did get the necessary plates and forks and enjoyed the curry before retiring to our hammocks, mentally preparing for the next day's showstopper.

Showstopper day went smoothly for most of us. As I have said, we had a bit of waiting time, which seemed to ease the pressure somewhat. There was nothing outstanding produced apart from Luis using gold leaf in finishing off his stuffed loaf and Martha turning out an amazing loaf, a bit like an octopus. It was beginning to look like Luis would be crowned Star Baker this week. I eventually confronted Mary and Paul with my stuffed loaf, quite a complex bake using eighteen different ingredients. I will admit that it looked a little plain; perhaps I should have brought some gold leaf and sparklers. I was not prepared to have it dismissed once more as being a bit plain and simple. Simple, I thought, and there is all that ingredients and skill hiding in there, just what are they expecting. I found out later that Jordan and myself were the two in danger of being sent home. They seem to have forgotten that my rolls were OK and I came fourth out of ten in the Technical and, of course, half the loaves produced were underbaked.

As I had forecast, Luis was made Star Baker and Jordan's journey was over, so I was spared for another week. The other bakers then departed for home with me off for another night in the Mercure. I had a pint or two in the downstairs bar and then found out that the only way I was going to get anything to eat was to go to my room and order something from the room service menu. This I duly did and ordered a sandwich, which cost me an additional £3 for delivery to my room, I didn't offer a tip as I had to wait for what seemed an age before it arrived. Incidentally, the origins of the word *tip* is an acronym of **To Insure Promptness**, from over one hundred years ago. I promptly ate the sandwich before retiring and looking forward to my flight on the Monday morning.

I made it home by lunchtime on the Monday and took Lucy out for a walk whilst I planned my practice for the following week. Week Four of the Bakeoff was puddings week and I felt I should straight away get in some baking in preparation. What I did do was make half a dozen of my Pear and Frangipane tarts, which are a favourite of Iris's. The recipe for these follows, the hint from Iris is to keep them until the day after they come out of the oven because they then taste better. I take the opposite view and prefer to eat them straight away. You could also have them warmed slightly and served with Crème Anglaise or whipped cream, making a superb pudding.

Pastry

Ingredients

150g plain flour

75g unsalted butter

75g caster sugar

3 large egg yolks

Frangipane

50g unsalted butter

50g caster sugar

1 large egg beaten

70g ground almonds

Few drops almond essence

1 x 410g tin pears halves in juice

You will also need 6 x 9-11 cm loose bottomed tart tins.

Method

Pastry

Add the flour & butter to a food processor & pulse for a few minutes until well mixed. Alternatively, just rub in the butter until it looks like crumbs then add the sugar and mix well. Finally bring the mix together with the three egg yolks. Wrap the paste in cling film and chill for 20 minutes. Be careful you don't over chill as the paste will crack very easily.

Once chilled, roll out the pastry to around the thickness of a pound coin. To prevent sticking it is best to use rice flour – much better than ordinary flour. Cut six rounds to fit your tart tins and pop in the refrigerator to chill whilst you make the frangipane.

Frangipane

Cream the butter and sugar until light and fluffy then add the ground almonds, beaten egg and almond essence, mixing well before dividing equally between the six tart tins.

Slice each pear half into 2mm slices and place one pear half on top of the frangipane on each of the six tarts. Heat oven to 185 degs C and bake the tarts until light brown – around 15 to 18 minutes. Once baked and cooled finish off with a light dusting of icing sugar. These are excellent eaten on the day but I have had reports of them being better after 24 hours.

Once you have made the frangipane using three egg yolks you will have three egg whites, ideal for making meringues. You do not need to make them straight away, as egg white will keep in the fridge in a sealed container for up to 14 days. For three egg whites, you will need approximately 200g caster sugar for your meringues, nothing else necessary. Allow the whites to reach room temperature and whisk the whites until just prior to stiff peak then add the sugar a teaspoon at a time. If you wish you could warm the sugar in the oven, this will assist in the dissolving process of the sugar in the egg white. Transfer to a piping bag and pipe on to baking parchment. Bake at 100 degrees C for 90 minutes then switch oven to off and leave them in until cool.

CHAPTER FOURTEEN

To Mrs Murphy's in East Ham

Back at the Wireless College after our continental adventure, I met up again with the other three and we swapped a tale or two about where we had been. Jeemsie Slater had a scare on two occasions when he was given a lift by what he thought were very strange men; however, he managed to keep his kilt on and escaped unscathed. I think I was lucky not to have had a similar experience but, of course, we were green in those days and did not have much idea of what was going on, still having a lot to learn about the wicked ways of the World. That was going to change of course, once I joined the Merchant Navy but for the moment all that was in the future. Before sailing off to the four corners of the World, it was a case of carrying on with the studies and continuing to enjoy life in Aberdeen. In 1963, we had a choice of seventeen cinemas in Aberdeen and at the weekends there was the dancing at the Beach Ballroom. On Sundays, there was always a concert at the Beach with famous names like The Springfield's, Eden Kane, Joe Brown & The Bruvvers, Johnny Kidd and The Pirates among the many names appearing there. Famously The Beatles appeared at a Sunday night concert in January 1963, I think we paid around three shillings (15p in today's money). Their performance was by no means outstanding; there may have been a problem with their equipment. At that time our own local group, Johnny & The Copycats, were far better. Only a few weeks after The Beatles appeared at the Beach they released Please Please Me, the rest is history. These acts were backed by the resident Johnny Scott Orchestra whose finale every Sunday was Rossini's William Tell Overture, or the theme from the Lone Ranger depending on which side of the musical fence you sat.

The Beach Ballroom was the venue for one of the student dances held each year, named The Battle. On 23rd November 1963, we were heading for The Battle at The Beach Ballroom via the Harriet Street Bar. We were upstairs in the bar quaffing a few pints when the news came through that President Kennedy had been assassinated in Dallas, Texas. There was a guy there playing the piano (this was pre-musak times) and he gave us a few bars of Yankee Doodle. They say everyone remembers where they were the night Kennedy was shot and that is certainly the case with me. As it happens, I was in Aberdeen on a training course in 1988 on the 25th anniversary of Kennedy's death and thought I would make my way along to the Harriet Street Bar and have a pint in honour and remembrance. After walking down Schoolhill I was devastated to find the Harriet no longer there, they had demolished it to make way for the new Bon Accord Shopping centre. All that remained was a pile of rubble, so I just had a piss round about where the toilets once stood and made my way to the Blue Lampie, hoping it had survived. If you visit Aberdeen today and decide to park in the Harriet Street Car Park, as you make your entrance you will be at the site of the front door of what was once the Harriet Street Bar.

A long winter's study led us to the first part of the final exams for the PMG Certificate, I was fortunate enough to pass the theoretical section without too much trouble. I also did quite well in the practical section apart from the part dealing with fault finding. This I fell down on, most likely due to lack of experience, but I resat the practical section of the exam in June and passed at the second attempt. The 12th of June 1964 saw me qualified as a Radio Officer. A total of eight finally passed out, from a starting class of twenty-eight. The difficulty for me arose when I tried to find employment, I was deemed too young. I had applied to several shipping companies as well as Marconi Marine, but they were the only Company to offer me some hope, saying that at age seventeen and six months I would be re-considered. I had no option but to wait. To pass the time I returned to College and studied for the First Class examination, passing the theoretical section by Christmas. I was due to take the practical part early in 1965, but received a letter from Marconi asking me to report to their Aberdeen Office for an interview.

The interview was a very informal affair; I just had to sit and listen to the depot manager telling me all about his career before being told I had a job and should now report to the company depot at Leith in Edinburgh. So at seventeen and a half I was off to Leith and received a short formal induction to The Marconi International Marine Communication Company and promptly onwards to East Ham in London where I was to be allocated to a ship. After a night in lodgings in Leith, I walked to Edinburgh Waverley Station and surrendered my travel warrant for a ticket to London. It is too late now to ask anyone but I never managed to figure out why I was sent to

Edinburgh in the first place, it was a bit of a wasted journey. At such a young age, you just do as you are told.

I was fortunate in having friends in London, our ex neighbours in Portknockie, Mr & Mrs Alexander had moved to London and lived in a house in Chigwell Road, South Woodford. My Mother had given me their telephone number so I let them know I was on my way and they said they would meet me at the South Woodford underground station. I was duly collected from the underground and spent the night in South Woodford before reporting to the Marconi depot in East Ham. Once I arrived at East Ham, I was told there was no ship for me but something was due to turn up in the next few days. Meantime, I was sent to Mrs Murphy's lodging house for a few days bed and breakfast, the charge Mrs Murphy made was one pound and sixpence per night. The breakfast was something I had never seen before, consisting of bacon, two eggs, sausage, beans, mushrooms and two rounds of fried bread. I did my best each morning with this massive feast but never finished one yet.

I spent the days in the waiting room at Marconi's office in East Ham, listening to tales from other Radio Officers coming and going from various ships in the London docks, eventually succumbing to the persuasive charms of the Union Man and joining the R.O.U. At lunchtimes, the entire office, led by Mr Stan Padfield, the Staff Clerk, repaired to the Cock Public House where they would drink pint after pint of ale. I hadn't come across lunchtime drinking before and declined the opportunity. Instead, I found a Wimpy Bar. I had never seen an eatery like this and I must say I really enjoyed lunchtimes there; it was all a big novelty to me. This short sojourn at East Ham ended when I was introduced to Mr R J Halpin, Radio Officer, who was just returning after a period of leave in his home town of Dublin. Mr Halpin was on his way to join an oil tanker, the Esso Portsmouth, and I was to accompany him as Junior Radio Officer. Before being allocated a ship on your own you had to complete six months as a junior with an experienced hand showing you the ropes.

Things started to get exciting for me when I found out the Esso Portsmouth was moored at Le Havre in France and we would have to fly across the channel to join her. Myself and Mr Halpin made our way to an old wartime airfield, RAF Manston, in Kent where we met the other members of the crew before boarding an old Dakota for my first ever flight in an aeroplane. The flight was uneventful and we duly boarded the Esso Portsmouth at the Esso refinery in Le Havre. First thing we all did was hand in our discharge books and sign the ships articles. After I was shown to my cabin I went to the saloon for lunch and was allocated my seat at the table with the three deck apprentices, quickly being informed that I was the youngest one on board. After lunch, I joined Mr Halpin in the Radio Room where he went over all the equipment and let me know exactly what my duties would be. In the evening, we sailed from Le Havre, bound for the oil terminal at Marsa el Brega in Libya North Africa.

The following morning we entered the Bay of Biscay and I sat down to breakfast at 8am. I was presented with a greasy plate of bacon and egg, due to us rolling in the deep, the egg was sliding all over the plate. A couple of mouthfuls saw me heading out of the saloon and yodelling down the big white microphone. That was the start of three days of mal de mer for me. They say if you are not sick when you first go to sea, there's something wrong with your head. I managed to confirm there was nothing wrong with my head, it took me three days to find my sea legs by which time we were only a day or so away from our destination in Libya. It was the French and not the Dundonians who invented marmalade as a cure for seasickness and named it mal-de-mer, which the English corrupted to marmalade. I do not think there is any cure for seasickness apart from sitting under a tree. However if you think you are going to suffer travel sickness at any time, eat oranges and apples as they taste the same coming up as going down!. There was no going ashore at Marsa el Brega, instead the ship dropped anchor and we connected to a pipeline coming out from the shore, and with a tugboat in attendance, we spent twenty-four hours loading our cargo of crude oil. I do not recall the name of the tug but do remember the radio call sign, MTFN.

From Brega we set course for the Esso refinery at Antwerp in Belgium, which had the deck apprentices a bit excited. They had spent the last few months between Brega and Fawley in England, so this was to be somewhere different for a change. We docked at Antwerp within the week and Mr Halpin gave me permission to go ashore, with all the warnings about behaving myself and letting me know I was still only seventeen. Some Belgian francs were collected from the ship's office and myself, two apprentices and three of the junior engineers set foot in my first foreign port – Antwerp.

We had a few beers and some sausage and frites with mayonnaise – you'll find the Belgians make the best frites ever, apparently they invented them – then we made our way to that favourite haunt of most British seamen in Antwerp, Danny's Bar in Skipper Street. This proved to be quite a revelation for me, it was a bit like the Kinks song, Lola – "she walked like a woman and talked like a man", most of the "women" in the bar were men. It was quite an education for a seventeen year old. Back on board ship we were underway before lunchtime, this time bound for Bandhar Mashur in Iran, through the Mediterranean, the Suez Canal, past Aden, through the Straits of Hormuz then up the Persian Gulf.

Seven days sailing took us to Port Said and the Suez Canal where we dropped anchor before joining the southbound convoy of ships the following morning at around 0430 hrs. A convoy system was in use for organisational and safety purposes, the route being almost a straight line south as far as Ismalia where the route doglegs to port before passing through the Bitter Lakes. The Lakes are where the northbound convoy of ships would drop anchor and await passage of the southbound convoy. A short journey from the Bitter Lakes led us to Ismalia before exiting the canal at Port Suez and into the heat of the Red Sea. At the southern end of the Red Sea, we entered the Gulf of Aden and stopped for a short while to load bunkers (fuel oil) before heading for the Straits of Hormuz and north to Bandar Mashur, not far from the Iraqi border, to load our cargo of crude oil. The heat was an incredible shock. We had no air conditioning and the humidity was worst whilst we were alongside loading oil, hardly any movement of air to give a breeze and any breeze we did get was a searing hot wind from across the desert. Whilst we were loading cargo, which took around thirty-six hours, the galley was shut down for safety reasons and all food served on board was cold. This made a pleasant change and because it was so hot, the cold food, salads etc., were much appreciated.

Fully loaded, we left port bound for somewhere in Europe. We did not know our exact destination at this time, the only message we received from Esso in London was L.E.F.O., which was Land's End for Orders. Once we had cleared the Straits of Gibraltar, we received firm orders to proceed to Kalundborg in Denmark to discharge. Kalundborg is a nice little town with an oil refinery on the opposite side of the island where Copenhagen is located. Once we had negotiated the Skagerrak and the Kattegat, we tied up alongside at the oil terminal. We had a good run ashore there, the only problem being that the Carlsberg Brewery in Denmark was on strike and with the beer being very scarce one had to buy a small glass of schnapps along with every beer. Yes, we had a great time there and as it was over the weekend, we went to a local dance on the Saturday night – more beer and schnapps. The local newsagent in Kalundborg did a roaring trade in magazine sales. Denmark was way ahead of the UK at that time and had many "Health & Efficiency" type magazines illustrating parts of the human anatomy, which had hitherto been a complete mystery to the average young chap. The best the UK could do at that time in the sixties was "Parade", "Spick & Span" or "Spanking Monthly". Quite a change for me as prior to this exposure I had always looked forward each month to getting the "Meccano Magazine" and "Practical Wireless!"

After thirty-six hours in Denmark, we were underway again, facing a twenty-one day voyage, if we kept our speed at around 14 knots. Our destination was Kharg Island back in the Persian Gulf where we were to load another cargo of crude oil. I was by now getting quite used to being at sea and we had a very pleasant voyage through the Mediterranean to Port Said and an uneventful passage through the Suez Canal. I say uneventful but once you had dropped anchor at Port Said, the bumboat men, arabs selling the usual Port Said souvenirs, besieged the ship. Camel stools, leather wallets, dirty postcards and the infamous Port Said Bibles (dirty books). Also coming on board with the bumboat men was the Gilly-Gilly man, really a magician who would try to show you all kinds of tricks; these tricks usually involved you parting with some silver at one stage or another. You never saw it again and quite often ended up with a chicken in your pocket instead. For those in need of a haircut we also welcomed on board "Scouse", an Egyptian barber who could converse using your particular accent. He kinda failed with me as the best he could do was a semi-Glaswegian patter – way off the Doric mark! – his speciality was the Liverpool accent, hence his nickname. Three weeks after leaving Denmark we tied up at Kharg Island and for the next thirty-six hours took on board a full load of Iranian crude oil. This time we discharged in the port of Hamburg in Germany. As most of the crew on board had now completed four months, it was time for them to go on leave. I had the opportunity to remain on articles for another three months but as Mr.Halpin was also going on leave I decided to sign off, have some leave and finish my six months as junior on another ship. We left the ship and were transported by bus to a small airfield near Hamburg from where we flew to Manston in Kent; we were then bussed to a hotel in London before travelling from Kings Cross to Aberdeen the following day, home for a spot of leave. I had packed a bottle of Four Bell's Rum prior to leaving the ship and also had two hundred Perfectos Finos cigarettes in my case for my Dad. On unpacking at home I found that both the rum and cigarettes were missing. For our journey from the ship to the airport in Germany our luggage had been transported in a separate wagon, whilst we journeyed in the bus. The only solution to the mystery of the missing rum and cigarettes was that the luggage had been ransacked by the Germans. Letters exchanged between myself and Mr Halpin revealed that he and a few others had found the same, and we thought the war was over!

After three weeks at home on leave I had a call from the Staff Clerk at Marconi's East Ham requiring me to report to London in order to join the SS Benmhor for a three month trip to complete my six months as junior R.O. I was quite excited about this as the Benmhor was one of The Ben Lines ships and they all did trips to the Far East, Malaysia, Hong Kong, Thailand and other exotic locations. Before heading East of Suez I'm going to let you have a recipe for a dish, which although quite simple, being the Chinese equivalent of the omelette, became a favourite of mine during my three months with the Ben Line, Prawn or Crab Foo Yung.

Prawn Foo Yung

Ingredients

100g prawns or white crab meat (fresh if you can get it but I have used canned)

4 large eggs

1 white onion

75g chesnut mushrooms

Handful of bean sprouts

Small bunch watercress

2 tbsps ground nut oil

Method

Slice the onion thinly and fry in a wok with groundnut oil until softened, add the mushrooms, bean sprouts and prawns then toss for two minutes. Beat the four eggs, season and add to the wok, mixing thoroughly with the other ingredients until cooked. Cook more as scrambled eggs rather than as an omelette. Season well with pepper and salt; add the watercress, mix and serve immediately accompanied by boiled rice. Have some light soy sauce on hand, in case you need additional flavour. However, I usually find the crab gives the right amount of taste to the dish. Foo Yong is sometimes served with an oyster sauce based accompaniment but I prefer it without. You could substitute the prawn with crab or shrimp, both equally tasty. As we had a Hong Kong crew on the Benmhor, Chinese food was a daily feature and gave us a chance to sample the real McCoy rather than the takeaways we get at today's Chinese restaurants in the U.K.

CHAPTER FIFTEEN

Week Four of The Bakeoff – Puddings

Week Four of the Bakeoff was Puddings Week and we were all looking forward to the Baked Alaska, at least we thought this is a different challenge. Once again, I flew down to Heathrow on the Friday evening, meeting the others at the Hotel Mercure. All nine of us, accompanied by Murray, had our twelve quids worth of food and drink at the La Tasca restaurant in Newbury. Much of the discussion that evening was around making ice cream and trying to guess what the Technical Bake would be.

Our brief for the Signature Bake had been to create eight self-saucing puddings. I studied this at home and first considered chocolate fondant puddings, one of my more successful desserts. After studying the instructions received from Chloe Avery, I had decided that chocolate fondants did not satisfy the brief and so I created my own self-saucing sticky toffee puddings. I had completed them twice at home and they had turned out very well with a superb sauce being created. So on the first day of this the fourth week we set out to make the eight puddings. I had bought eight identical dishes especially for the job, which went very well, the only snag being that they left it so long before judging them that my cream topping had melted in the heat of the tent. The result was still an excellent dessert with a beautiful sauce, which met with Mary's approval, but with the melted cream they did not look very appetising. I tried to pass them off to Paul as "Cappuccino" style puddings but he just laughed and said he would give me extra points for thinking on my feet. What did surprise me was the fact that some of my colleagues had produced chocolate fondant desserts and they won the day with those – I had it wrong again!

Martha did very well with the self-saucing caper as she had produced "Key-Lime" puddings. You ought to have seen the smile on the judge's faces when she first said "Key-Lime", I thought they were about to cry with joy. Ryan Chong had made a Key Lime Pie in Series Three and that had been adjudged by Mary to be the best bake ever in the GBBO. I considered changing my Showstopper to a Key Lime Baked Alaska, pity I was too late to order up some limes. If anyone is planning entering the Bakeoff, you won't go far wrong with Key Lime.

Never mind, we had the ice cream making to look forward to the next day. It looked very much like the judges had not been very strict with their interpretation of the brief or I had not studied it very well myself. I was looking forward to having one of my puddings when I returned to the tent after lunch but they were all gone, scoffed by the crew!

The afternoon's Technical Bake was revealed to be a Tiramisu. I had never made one, nor had I ever eaten one. My remarks at the time were that I could not even spell it. I had originally thought this was a dish of Greek origin but apparently it is Italian. I succeeded with most parts of baking the Tiramisu but underestimated the amount of liquid to be poured into the cake (I disbelieved the recipe, it's supposed to very sappy!). The result was a dry Tiramisu earning me a placing of second last. However, I thought I had a good chance of making up lost ground with the Baked Alaska challenge scheduled for the following day. I was especially eager to try out the ice cream machines they said they had obtained for us. At home, I just had the cheaper version where you have to freeze the mixing bowl overnight. Although primitive it worked very well, producing a superb ice cream. It was the Andrew James model, cost me less than £30, and pur- chased especially for the Bakeoff. I just hoped that the machines we would be using for the Showstopper would function as well. We had a few drinks back at the Mercure that night and as the hotel bar was still being refurbished, once more the only food available were sandwiches via room service. I made do with a packet of crisps, which I munched whilst dreaming of my sticky toffee puddings! It was either crisps, nuts or those revolting Nacho things, which can only be likened to fried bus tickets.

Into the tent in the morning where there was no need to switch on the ovens for warmth, at 9am it was already 20 degrees C and with the sun shining in the sky it looked like we were going to have a scorcher. About time, I thought as I was missing Buckie's Mediterranean climate. No, the other bakers did not believe me either, but joking aside, we do experience generally nice weather along the Moray coast, getting no extremes. We normally escape the rainfall of the west coast of Scotland and seldom get any appreciable falls of snow in the wintertime. The only time it gets cold is when we have a northerly wind, which blows all the way from the Arctic Circle and chills you to the bone. However, as our friend Billy Connolly says; *"It's never the wrong weather, just the wrong clothes"*. If you are reading this from anywhere other than the Northeast of Scotland I would urge you to pay us a visit sometime, Billy Connolly can miss out Banff if he likes. The place is still generally unspoiled and unlike the Edinburgh's of this World, you will not be confronted with hordes of Japanese tourists or forests of tartan and bagpipes, it is also not unknown to find yourself with a whole beach all to yourself and there is even more of it to enjoy when the tide is out. We do not have a Ben Nevis up here but the Bin Hill overlooking Cullen and Portknockie is a nice climb for a picnic on a sunny day. If you do happen to ascend the Bin Hill please remember to bring a large stone with you, we are rebuilding the cairn at the summit, the original having been vandalised some years ago.

Paul and Mary, escorted by the makeup team and with Mel and Sue, confronted us at around 11am. I think the heat was getting to them; it was approaching 25 degrees C in the tent. Paul appeared tired, perhaps a heavy night and Mary was looking a wee bit wabbit. Mel and Sue were their usual jovial selves, jesting around the tent and doing a good job, getting us in a relaxed mood. It was good to have a wee bit of a laugh first thing as we were facing a gruelling five hours, and with the temperature looking as if it might rise further it was essential we keep our cool. Good humour, I feel, is an absolute essential in helping you cope with the trials of life. We all appreciate a good joke or funny story but now the bakers are getting used to me and every time I try to tell them something, they think it is another joke coming. I think I got away with it the first two or three weeks but now we are all getting to know the ins and outs of each other. One thing we all have in common is a sense of humour, not so much common sense really but I think the sense of humour more important. I am not sure if many people have any common sense today, maybe it is as my Mam used to say, *"The trouble with common sense is that it is not very common"*. I think she was right. Then again, she was right about most things, trouble is you do not appreciate the truth in that until you have reached the age your mother was when she said it. By then it is generally too late for your life to profit from the knowledge.

On with the show then, the Showstopper that is. First task was to make the ice cream and in order to kick that off I had to create a custard and allow it to cool. Once the custard was completed and cool, I mixed it with double cream and vanilla essence. I had considered adding flavouring but personally, I only like vanilla ice cream. The mix was transferred to the ice cream machine and I got on with baking my flan case and preparing to make the Italian meringue, which was to form the outside of the "Alaska". As it was around twenty years since I had made a Baked Alaska, the task turned out to be a very nostalgic experience and despite the heat inside the tent, I enjoyed every minute of the process. I was fortunate in that the sponge flan base for my Alaska had turned out well, just like a bought one. The Italian meringue also turned out perfectly, all I had to do then was assemble the various parts as soon as the ice cream was finished and had had enough time in the freezer to solidify properly.

At this stage, around four hours into the process there seemed to be nothing but panic ensuing in the tent. Everyone seemed to be blaming the heat of the day for slowing the ice cream making, with some transferring his or her ice creams from one freezer to another in a bid to speed up the freezing. I kept my ice cream in the freezer trying not to look at it too often and eventually I found it had frozen quite well. I sat down with a small bowl of ice cream at this stage and thoroughly enjoyed it. Just the ticket on such a hot and busy day. At what I thought was the correct time I assembled the Alaska, complete with the strawberries and strawberry coulis inside. After finishing off the outside with the Italian meringue, I piped on a pink and blue design. I had originally intended to make the Alaska as a model of a woman and had a porcelain figurehead to top off my design with. However, I was told I could not use this figurehead, they said for copyright(?) reasons. It was actually an antique cake decoration I had inherited from my Mother, mais c'est la vie.

Quite a few of the others appeared to be having problems getting their ice creams to freeze properly, resulting in some of them having to present to the judges what appeared to be a soggy mess. Fortunately, Paul and Mary had realised that we had had a very tough time indeed in fulfilling the requirements of the Showstopper Bake (owing to the heat of the day) and were very sympathetic in their summing up of the "bakes" presented to them. That is until I marched forward proudly with my effort. Mary said there was not enough flavour – it was vanilla, adding that there did not seem to be enough fruit inside it (250g strawberries, she never looked). To begin with, Paul said my sponge flan was good, the ice cream was also good and the Italian meringue was OK, he then completed his criticism by saying that I was so safe, I was beginning to

147

fail and that I was missing the point. I disagreed with that statement saying that it was not my turn to miss the point as I had missed it yesterday.

Apart from the criticisms aimed at my Baked Alaska, the only other one the judges disapproved of was Iain's. He had lost it in the heat of the moment (or the heat of the tent if you like) and binned his ice cream after it had been inadvertently left outside the freezer in the hot tent air for a while. I had heard something going on behind me and the first I knew of a problem was when Iain marched out of the tent. That is about as much as I recall about the notorious "bin-gate" affair, but I cannot help but think that Iain's actions had saved the day for me. If Iain had been like a few other bakers and presented even a partially or fully melted Alaska, then it would have been me saying arrivederci in the fourth week. As it was, Iain unfortunately had to go back across the sea to Ireland. This was a great pity as Iain was a very likeable chap and I think Paul was genuinely sad to let him go, as he had appeared to have set his sights on my departure that day.

The other bakers bade their farewell and made their respective ways home whilst I returned to the Mercure for a relaxing evening before heading for Heathrow and back to Buckie on the Monday morning. As it had been a splendid day weather-wise, I had a nice walk in the evening of the Berkshire countryside before ending the day in the downstairs bar, clutching a pint of Nelson, wondering whether to have a bag of nuts or crisps. The nuts won and I scoffed them and another pint before retiring to my hammock and I must say, slept like a baby, yes I wet the bed again! No, not true, but I just could not resist that.

Arriving home at midday on the Monday I decided to have an easy week, feeling I did not need to practise any more pie making, which was the theme for the upcoming Week Five. The only pie I made that week was a Lemon-Meringue Pie, one of my favourites from my childhood, Iris does not like it very much but I went ahead and made one anyway. Just in case you ever fancy one yourself, Dear Reader, I have included the recipe here. I know it is a very simple pie but give it a go sometime, I am sure you will enjoy it. Most LMP recipes stipulate two or more lemons; my recipe uses only one but still has a sharp lemon flavour and makes a great pudding for five or six people.

Lemon Meringue Pie

Ingredients

The Pastry Case

150g plain flour

75g butter

75g caster sugar

3 large egg yolks

The Filling

2 large eggs

250g caster sugar

1 lemon

150ml water

25g cornflour

Method

For the pastry case, rub the butter in to the flour, either by hand or by pulsing in a food processor.Add the 75g caster sugar then bring the paste together with the three egg yolks. Wrap in cling film and chill for 20 minutes. Be careful not to over-chill as it may then crack too easily.

Once pastry is chilled, roll out and line an 18cm flan tin. As this is a pate sucre or sweet pastry, I find it rolls out much easier if you use rice flour to stop it sticking to your work surface. It is difficult to handle but the bonus is it does not shrink and it never gives you a soggy bottom. Bake blind at 190 degrees C for 15 minutes then remove your beans or whatever you bake blind with and reduce oven to 150 degs c. for a further five minutes

Separate the eggs and add the yolks to the water together with the lemon zest, juice and 100g of the caster sugar before bringing to the boil. Add the cornflour dissolved in a little water and stir until thickened. Pour this filling into the flan case and make the meringue. You could just make meringue with the two egg whites but remember you have three egg whites left over from the pastry making. It might be a good idea to make a larger batch of meringue and use the surplus for small meringues or a Pavlova. However, the spare whites will keep for up to two weeks covered in the refrigerator. Whisk the egg white until stiff and then add the remaining caster sugar, one teaspoon at a time. Spoon or pipe the meringue over the lemon filling and bake at 150 degrees C for 25 minutes or until the meringue is firm and has browned slightly. Alternatively, you could bake the meringue at 100 degs C for ninety minutes if you prefer a white meringue. The pie in the picture has had the meringue baked for 90 minutes at 100 degs C so it is lovely and crisp with a non-chewy inside. Nice on its own or with a little cream.

Just add a little cream

CHAPTER SIXTEEN

Bound for The Orient

Once I had reported to the Marconi Marine Office in East Ham, the Staff Clerk sent me to the Benmhor at King George V dock in London. I got a lift to the docks from one of the service engineers who had a job to do at the docks, so thankfully I did not end up on public transport and have to walk with all my kit. On arrival at KG V, I reported to the Chief Radio Officer on board the Benmhor, Mr J R Crockett, from Aberdeen. It was a relief for me to hear a "home voice", as on board my previous ship I was the only one of Scottish nationality. In fact, almost all the Ben Line Employees, apart from the Chinese crew, were Scottish with the majority originating from the East Coast of Scotland. The only exceptions were a few engineers hailing from the Northeast of England, bringing their experience from the shipyards surrounding Newcastle. As a rule, the Ben Line did not employ any personnel hailing from the West of Scotland.

SS Benmhor

Mr Crockett took me on a tour of the Benmhor where I met most of the other officers and Chinese crew on board, and then it was into the Radio Room for the rest of the day. The Benmhor was a relatively old ship so the radio room equipment held no surprises for me. I was then given the schedule for the voyage; it was to last three months and six days. The full voyage being: Port Said for Suez Canal transit, Aden in The Yemen for Bunkers, Port Swettenham, Penang, Singapore, Bangkok, Rejang in Borneo, Cebu in The Philippine's, Hong Kong, Singapore, Port Swettenham, Aden for bunkers, Suez Canal Transit, finally returning to the U.K. and docking at Liverpool. I was looking forward to Borneo, as a child I had quite often listened to my grandfather's song about "The Wild Man of Borneo". This song, along with a passionate recital of Tennyson's "The Charge of The Light Brigade" were his party pieces. The last time I recall him performing both of these was at my sister's wedding reception in Cullen Town Hall when I was eleven. I think he had consumed more than a glass or two of rum.

We were due to sail from London on the following afternoon's tide and in the evening Mr Crockett, myself and the second engineer went ashore and had a pint or two of Watney's Red Barrel, which appeared to be the fashionable drink in those days. Returning before ten, I went to my cabin and had a very sound sleep before being roused at 0700 with a cup of tea by the Chinese steward who looked after myself along with the refrigeration and junior engineers. Once I had showered and had breakfast I went to the Radio Room and tuned in to the latest weather report, passing this to the third mate who was on the bridge busy making preparations for our afternoon sailing. I found out from the third mate that the passengers were due on board just before lunch and that we would have our full complement of twelve, all of them bound for Singapore. In addition to the passengers, we had a large cargo of munitions for the British Army at Singapore and a large selection of goods to be discharged at various ports in the Far East. At noon, I tuned in to Rugby Radio, received the time signal, and checked the ship's chronometer, making careful note of the chronometer gain/loss in the notebook. This was to be one of my important tasks in the days work, knowledge of the exact time at Greenwich was essential in establishing the ship's longitude.

On board the Benmhor 1965

The SS Benmhor was a steamship originally built in 1949 for the Lancashire Shipping Company and named the Penrith Castle; bought by the Ben Line in 1952 she was renamed Benmhor. When the Penrith Castle first sailed in 1949 she had on board a refrigeration Engineer by the name of Dai Hughes (he was Welsh funnily enough) so when the Ben Line bought her they also took over the refrigeration engineer along with the ship and he had been on board ever since. As the Benmhor only carried a refrigerated cargo about once a year, old Dai had an easy time of it on-board. Most of his time was spent drinking beer. The beer we had on board was the half pint tins of Tennent's lager, in the red and gold cans and in those days we required use of the "top-end spanner" to open them, no ring-pulls in those days. There was a bar on board the ship but access was restricted to the passengers and senior officers. Our cabins had no refrigerator, and anyone requiring a cold beer had to press the bell in the cabin and the steward would bring one along. Normally, six rings got you six cans if you had a guest or two, whilst any "party" on board would require a whole case of twenty-four; in order to get a case just one very long press of the bell was all that was necessary. I think old Dai must have worn out his bell, it seemed to me that he opened a can every thirty minutes or so. My own cabin was next door to his and I could hear the top-end spanner in action most of the day and into the night.

We headed down river at noon, dropping off the Thames pilot at Sheerness before turning south at Ramsgate and then heading west through the English Channel. A smooth passage in the English Channel was followed by more calm seas as we navigated through the Bay of Biscay before passing Cape Trafalgar and very soon after, we had Gibraltar on the port side. That was almost five days after leaving London, as the engine was getting on a bit we only managed twelve knots. Another week of sunny days and calm seas saw us enter Port Said for a transit of the Suez Canal. Aden was our next port of call, but just to take on some fuel for the rest of the trip to the east. That was a very hot thirteen hundred miles, taking us just over four days. Air conditioning would have been a bonus but we had to make do with whatever breeze blew through the accommodation. We had to drink more than a few cold beers as the on-board water tasted a bit like weasel piss.

Our twelve passengers were beginning to feel the heat and things promised to get even hotter as we made our way across the Indian Ocean. One of the main advantages of travelling to warmer climes by sea is that you experience a gradual exposure to the heat of the sun and you very quickly adapt to the increase in temperature. Our passage after leaving Aden was east across the Indian Ocean, passing to the north of the island of Socotra. Socotra was the name of the first ship that Mr.Crockett had sailed on, just after the war started in 1939. He named his new house in Aberdeen after the island and had a sign made in the shape of the island. More than 25% of the unusual plant species found on Socotra are unique to the island. Ten days later, we were picking up the pilot before docking at Penang in Malaysia. After Penang, a half days sailing saw us all ashore, and paying a visit to the Jungle Bar in Port Swettenham, an infamous haunt amongst sailors to the Far East. Incidentally, Port Swettenham was renamed Port Kelang and is the port of call for cruise ships for trips to the Malaysian capital city, Kuala Lumpur. British Empire builder Frank Swettenham had the port named after himself in the late 19th century.

Less than another day sailing and we dropped the hook in the Singapore Roads and commenced transferring cargo via lighter. We had the British Army on board to supervise the unloading of the munitions cargo we had for them. It has to be said they did not do too much supervising, spending the days having a beer or two with us as their hosts. We spent one evening at the Sergeants Mess, RAF Seletar, as guests of the army. One of the older soldiers told us he remembered sitting there as the Japs advanced across the cricket field. He had then ended up in Changi where he spent the rest of the war and unlike a great deal of his colleagues, he survived and remained in the army after the war had ended.

Singapore was a great run ashore in those days, a few drinks in the Cellar Bar before heading down Bugis Street (pronounced Boogie) for some chow. One dish I enjoyed in Singapore was satay chicken or pork, after a few Tiger beers you were never sure if it was chicken, pork or maybe something else. It did not seem to matter then, a bit like kebabs in this country; however, I have never been that drunk that I have eaten one of them. Fortunately, I am not too fussy regarding food, unlike my wife Iris, who won't eat anything that flies in the air or lives in a hole in the ground. Today, pork or chicken satay is still one of my favourites. At midnight on Bugis Street the Kai Tais or Beaney Boys would arrive, another revelation. These "ladies" would parade as if in a fashion show, up and down Bugis Street. They were actually transvestite men and very popular with the sailors, soldiers and tourists. I think Bugis Street, as it was, lasted into the seventies when the Singaporean authorities "cleaned the place up". I visited Singapore in 2005 and was disappointed to find the old Singapore had disappeared along with the Kai Tais, monsoon drains and the smells of the Orient. That's progress for you, today you can visit Singapore, Hong Kong, New York, London, Paris or any large city and find little to distinguish one from the other. Today Singapore is all skyscrapers and the whole place is immaculately clean. Sadly, no longer will Jack ashore be dining in Bugis Street or falling into monsoon drains, as he attempts to stagger back to his ship.

When I think back to my time at sea, I always remember Singapore and especially the smells when you walked ashore at night, the taste of the street food and Tiger Beer. Mr.Crockett had been going ashore in Singapore for years, was excellent company and a fantastic guide to all the sights and sounds of the east. Change Alley was one place he took me to; a large market where it was the normal practice to haggle before paying for anything you bought. Things have changed these days. On a recent visit to Singapore on the P&O Cruise ship Oriana. I thought I might buy a Rolex watch ashore and tried to haggle the price; the salesman just looked at me as if I had cloven feet and refused to budge a cent. I still wear my Rotary; it was a fraction of the cost and is very accurate. On departure from Singapore, we had just over two and a half days at sea before tying up in Bangkok. We had an excellent berth just beside the dock gates and not far from the Mariners Club where they had a swimming pool with an external bar in a shady spot beside the pool. This is where I had my first ever Seven-Up, in a tall glass with crushed ice and a slice of lime, an excellent drink in the heat of a Bangkok noon. I was beginning to feel like James Bond. We preferred to leave the beer until the evening and we did not have far to go for that either. Next door to the Mariners was the Mosquito Bar, and I remember another nearby called the OK Bar. There was one at the end of the block called the Venus Room, if I remember correctly? Just beside the Venus was the Temple Bar. I remember my Father's Auntie asking me if I had seen the temples in Bangkok, I said I had seen the Temple Bar! If you lasted as far as that one there was always the Golden Gate on the other side of the road, a more upmarket joint where the bar flies were all in uniform with white blouses and red bow ties.

The Mossie, probably the most famous seaman's bar in the World

Our next port of call was another jewel in the Far East, Hong Kong. This was where some of the ship's company assembled by the gangway, waiting for a taxi to take them to see the quack. Crockett told me they called this the "drip parade", adding that they may have caught something from a "toilet seat" in Port Swettenham or Bangkok, having failed to deploy the "sporting gear".

To reach Kowloon from Hong Kong you can board the Star Ferry, which runs frequently between the mainland and Hong Kong Island. The ferry fare here in 1964 was only twenty HK cents. With there being at that time sixteen HK$ to the pound, this meant that the ferry fare in Sterling was only three pence in old money, approximately 1.2p in our present day decimal currency. This made the Star Ferry the cheapest fare in the world in 1964. If you visit Hong Kong, when boarding or disembarking the Star Ferry, look for the plaques indicating that the landing stages were made by Hall Russell Aberdeen and that is Aberdeen Scotland not Hong Kong.

Mr.Crockett took me on my first run ashore in Hong Kong and after a quick sight-seeing tour we boarded the ferry for Kowloon where he had to see the chap he had ordered a camphorwood chest from the previous trip. We then paid a visit to the tailor, Mr.Lo and I was measured for a suit, Mr.Lo promised to have it ready for the following day, if I returned for a fitting in the evening. In Buckie at that time, we still had two shops where you could order a tailor-made suit, Burtons and Claude Alexander, and they would take anything up to six weeks to deliver a suit. True to his word, Mr Lo had the suit ready the next day and it fitted perfectly, with a label inside stating that it was *"Especially Made for Mr Norman Calder by Wan Hung Lo, Tailor Kowloon"*. The suit was single breasted in a light grey wool, I thought light grey would show off my suntan and I would look good for the chicks when I went home on leave. I still have the jacket hanging in my wardrobe but it has shrunk and no longer fits me.

Most seamen visiting Hong Kong got a suit or a jacket made to measure, they did not take long to make, and were reasonably priced. Besides the suit, most of us also bought underpants at $1HK per pair and socks at much the same price. The brand was always "Hings Ballbags" but they did not last too long. Generally, we just wore them until they were rotten, and then consigned them to the bin.

Next port of call was Rejang in Borneo where we managed to load a large number of teak logs, without seeing the Wild Man, then stopping off at Cebu in the Phillipines to load locally crafted furniture for the UK. Our return voyage took us back to Hong Kong, Singapore, Port Swettenham, Penang and Aden for fuel before another Suez Canal transit, finally docking in Liverpool exactly three months and six days after sailing down the Thames. We had a good run ashore in Liverpool where all the lassies looked like Cilla Black and nearly all the lads were sporting what might have passed for a Beatles style haircut. Of course, I was just as guilty myself, having already consigned my jar of Brylcreem to the bin. Next day we signed off articles and Mr. Crockett and I reported to the Marconi Marine depot in Liverpool. Crockett was off home for a few weeks leave before returning to the Benmhor after she had done her tour of continental ports. Marconi had organised a month long radar maintenance course for me in Cardiff, after which they would send me on a ship on my own as Radio Officer in charge. First, It was off home for a short spell of leave.

Whilst at sea, no matter which ship you were on, three o'clock in the afternoon was always "Tea and Tabnabs" time. Always tea, never coffee and Tabnabs were whatever cake, biscuit or fancy piece the cook had managed to prepare that day. My favourite was always shortbread which most sea cooks were capable of turning out, albeit in various shapes and styles. Before getting back to the Bakeoff, I will let you have my own recipe for shortbread, which is a light open biscuit. I have always found it to be very popular with most people. You may well ask why it is called short "bread" when it is not bread but a biscuit. The reason for that is because around a couple of centuries ago, there was a tax on biscuits and to overcome this in Scotland they renamed their favourite biscuits as a type of bread – shortbread to avoid the tax. Now you know.

Shortbread Biscuits

Ingredients

225g butter

100g caster sugar

225g plain flour

85g fine semolina (Marshalls Farola is best)

½ tsp salt

Rice flour for dusting

Cream the butter and sugar until light and fluffy using a stand mixer or by hand.

Sieve together the flour, semolina and salt before mixing with the creamed sugar and butter until well combined.

Dust the dough with a little rice flour, wrap in cling film or a food bag and chill for 15 minutes.

Set oven to 170 degs C

After 15 minutes, dust your work surface with rice flour and roll out the dough to approximately 5mm thick, prick the surface all over with a fork or docker. Cut out biscuits using a 2-1/2" fluted cutter (6cm) and transfer to a parchment lined baking tray using a palette knife. Re-roll cuttings and repeat. Bake for approximately 17 minutes but do not allow to brown.

Remove from oven when done, dust with caster sugar and place on cooling rack using a palette knife as they are very soft at this stage.

Keep these in a sealed container before eating; they seem to improve in flavour after a week or so.

Notes on shortbread

Never use cornflour in your shortbread and forget about the suggestion of some recipes that you use vanilla essence. They should only taste of butter and for that reason only use quality butter and never vegetable fat or margarine.

I have made these with 50g of porridge oats in place of 50g of the flour and have done something similar using ground almonds; both of these work very well.

They make a nice treat with a squirt of whipped cream topped with a strawberry or raspberry.

Total time: 45 minutes

Total cost: around £2.20 and makes approximately thirty-two biscuits.

Shortbread

CHAPTER SEVENTEEN

Week Five of The Bakeoff – Pies

The week we had all been waiting for was upon us – Pie Week. Not only pies but the Showstopper, requiring a tower of three pies, sweet or savoury; any kind you like and any pastry you care to choose. All of us, or rather all that was left of us, met up again on the Friday night, ready to kick off Week 5. A Siamese Restaurant was the chosen venue this time so we gathered in the Art of Siam and had a drink and a chat. We settled down and had an excellent plate of Thai nosh. Once we had eaten, each one of us had to pay our own bill – that was why they gave us the £12 per diem. This occasion was no exception and Diana was at the bar with some of the other ladies waiting her turn to pay. That is when it happened; Diana fainted and went down like a sack of spuds, striking her head quite badly on the hard stone floor. Our chaperone, Murray Grindon phoned for an ambulance, which arrived in about five minutes. Basingstoke Hospital kept Diana in overnight for observation.

She then had to be withdrawn from the Great British Bakeoff, which must have been a source of great disappointment to her. Certainly, we were very sorry to hear she would not be joining us on the Saturday morning for the start of Pie Week. Naturally, every cloud has a silver lining and we thought pity about Diana but on a more positive note, they probably will not be sending anyone home this week. I think we then all took our foot off the gas; certainly, I approached the tent on Saturday morning with a more casual attitude than was normal. First task on the Saturday morning after the usual round of coffee and trips to the tent, we had the Signature Bake to complete. This one was for a custard tart; I made the usual mistake of taking the request too literally and made just a plain custard tart. Some of the others decorated theirs with fruit and Luis especially made a beautiful job of his Manchester Tart, the top being finished off with mango and syphilis fruit. Mine in comparison looked rough, although the taste was superb.

The afternoon's exercise was the Technical Challenge and turned out to be something no one foresaw, we had to make some rough puff pastry and use it to cover poached pears. We made the pastry and whilst it was chilling, peeled and poached the pears. Although quite straightforward, the pears challenge proved not as easy for some and I managed to come out best of the boys in the final judging. One of them had a real bit of bad luck and all the pastry fell off his pears, getting him last place in the Technical Challenge, not a good position to be in.

So it was that I steamed into the tent on the Sunday morning supremely confident in a positive conclusion to the day. This was for two reasons; one I had done reasonably well in the Technical and two, with Diana now in hospital we all felt certain that week five would see nobody dismissed. My original plan for my tower of pies was to have been a steak and ale pie on the bottom, a fish in cheese pie in the middle, topped off with a lemon meringue pie. However, in an effort to be more adventurous I changed the bottom pie to a venison, haggis and spinach pie and the top one to a raspberry and passion fruit pie, topped with Italian meringue. I had found a bottle of lavender flavour and used that to flavour the Italian meringue, thinking that would be a tad more exotic.

At the end of the five-hour Showstopper, we all marched up with our towers of pies and I strode forward at the appointed time, proudly displaying my "Pieffel Tower". I had used three different types of pastry for my Showstopper and felt that that may well get me extra points as most of the other contestants had made their pies using hot water crust. Paul would condemn this, I thought, as being too "safe". How wrong was I, they did not like the lavender flavour of the meringue, and after ignoring the fish pie they said that the venison and haggis pie was too dry. Despite turning out three different types of pastry, I felt they had given me little or no credit for my efforts. After the judges' comments on my Showstopper, I was beginning to get the feeling that the game was up for me and was only consoled by the fact that some of the other Bakers appeared to be in a more precarious position with burnt pies, leaking pies and less than perfect pears.

That second day came to a close and we were arranged in the usual semi-circle all ready to receive the judges' decision. Kate, I thought, had seemed to live her life like a candle in the wind but today her flame burned brightly and she was declared Star Baker – well done Kate! I was then surprised and disappointed to hear my name announced as the person chosen to depart the tent. This was the end of the road for me, Adios, Cheerio, Auf viedersehn, Sayonara, Au revoir, Toodle pip, Arivaderci, Good-bye. I was stunned and so was everyone else I think. Murray congratulated me on accepting the decision with good grace. I was naturally a wee bit cheesed off at the time, as I had thought we were all safe. Looking back now, I consider myself extremely fortunate to have been picked for the Bakeoff in the first place. My feeling was that I had done well to make it all the way to Week Five. By no stretch of the imagination was my baking talent in the same league as the others, but I did think Lady Luck had smiled on me, for a short while anyway. Everyone else went off to board trains at Newbury Railway Station or drive home; I went back to the Mercure and consoled myself with a few pints of Stella Artois. I did not need to order any food from room service as I had a bagful of bits of pork pies that I had managed to scrounge from the tent as my own pies had disappeared. The pork pie bits were cold and didn't look very appealing, but I was hungry. Early next morning the limo picked me up, took me to Heathrow and I was homeward bound once more but not for the last time as we still had the Extra Slice programme to do, together with the Bakeoff Final and the Final Extra Slice.

I will let you know all about the final of The Bakeoff and the Extra Slice programmes in the following chapter; I think I enjoyed that bit more than the Bakeoff itself.

Meantime, I thought you might appreciate having a look at a vegetarian recipe. I have to do this one every Christmas Day, as Corinne, Louise and John are vegetarians. I must admit that although I am not a veggie, I do enjoy it myself.

167

Vegetarian Nut Roast Wellington

Nut Roast Mixture:

1 onion, finely chopped

1 tbsp olive oil

200g whole mixed nuts

175g fresh wholemeal breadcrumbs

75g mature cheddar, grated

200ml vegetable stock

1 egg, beaten

½ tsp Marmite

1 tsp dried oregano

25g dried cranberries

500g pack of ready-made puff pastry or make your own if you have time

1 egg beaten

Mushroom Duxelles:

250g chestnut mushrooms, very finely chopped

1 shallot, finely chopped

few fresh thyme leaves

25g butter

For the Mushroom Duxelles:

Sweat the mushrooms, thyme and chopped shallot in the butter over a very low heat until all the liquid has evaporated and what remains is an almost dry mushroom pate. Set aside to cool.

For the Nut Roast:

Sauté the chopped onion in the olive oil, then set aside to cool.

Grind the nuts in a food processor until reasonably fine, but still with some texture. Place the groundnuts in a large bowl; add the breadcrumbs, grated cheddar, oregano and cooled onion; mix well. (At this point, you can put it in the fridge and finish it on the day, if you want.) Whisk the stock together with the beaten egg and Marmite; add this to the bowl and mix with a fork until the mixture starts to hold together. Remove about 1/3 of the mixture to a small bowl and stir in the dried cranberries.

Assembling the Wellington:

Unroll the pastry onto a lightly floured surface and roll lightly with a rolling pin to make it a bit larger. You need to make it approximately 12" x 10" but check the size of your Wellington and make sure there is enough pastry to enclose it completely.

Put the nut roast mixture with cranberries in the centre of the pastry and form into a rough rectangle about 8" x 3.5" x 3.5".Spread the mushrooms duxelles over the top, then cover with the remaining nut roast mixture.....OR as I sometimes do...... Mould the wellington and chill before wrapping in pastry. Make a rectangle around 1" high with the cranberry mix, cover with the duxelle then the main part of the nut roast (this is it upside down.) This makes a nice squared rectangular shape. You should end up with the Nut Roast Mixture, The Mushroom Duxelles and on top the Nut Roast and Cranberry mix.

Chill.

Place the nut roast upside down on your pastry sheet. Fold the edges of the pastry over like a parcel, completely enclosing the nut roast, using the beaten egg to seal all the edges. You may need to cut off a bit of the pastry to avoid the seams being too thick. Decorate with shapes from the remaining pastry. Brush with beaten egg and finish off the top with sea salt and dried oregano.

Tip: If you want a very even glaze, pass your beaten egg through a sieve before using and add 1 tsp water with a pinch salt. This gets rid of the chakalaka - the membrane that links the yolk and white so giving a smoother, more even glaze. In some parts of the country, the chakalaka is known as the chalaza. In South Africa, the chakalaka is a spicy vegetable dish.

Line a shallow baking tray with non-stick baking paper and, very carefully, turn the Wellington over and lay it, seam-side down, on the baking tray. Brush all over with the rest of the beaten egg and bake at 210C for 20 minutes then turn the temperature down to 180C and cook for a further 35-40 minutes until deep golden brown and cooked through. (I have a fan oven so you may need to adjust timings or temperatures a bit).

Rest for 20 minutes before serving.

For gravy, fry an onion and stir in 2 tbsps flour then deglaze with 250ml red wine, add some vegetable stock and reduce a bit. Pass through a sieve then continue to reduce the gravy.

Once gravy is as thick as you require add some redcurrant jelly to taste.

That well-known vegetarian and star of the Bakeoff, Iain Watters, has tested this recipe and found it to be superb.

CHAPTER EIGHTEEN

The Final of The Bakeoff & The Extra Slice

I The Final

Following my elimination from the Bakeoff and after relaxing at home for a few weeks, Mrs C, the family and myself were invited to attend the Final of the Bakeoff at the Tent in Welford Park. As this was a 625 mile journey, we made the decision to take the caravan and spend a few days near London. Lucy joined us in the car when we set off a few days beforehand and pitched up at the Caravan Club Site in Welwyn Garden City. This site is very handy for access to London as the train journey is only twenty-five minutes or so from Kings Cross, so was very convenient for us going to see the girls in Stoke Newington. The Bakeoff Final was a grand occasion, organised by Love Productions, and they had invited everyone involved with the Bakeoff production for the day out to watch the final. This included all the contestants plus all the film and production crews together with their families. I think we had over two hundred at Welford Park where the sun shone all day and we had a splendid picnic with the added pleasure for everyone of meeting Paul and Mary, along with Mel and Sue. As this was still the month of June and the programme due to broadcast in August, each invitee had to sign a form stating that they would not divulge any information about the Bakeoff and, in particular, who had won.

The three finalists were Richard, Luis and Nancy. They asked me who the winner might be and I said it would be close but if asked to wager I would have a bet on Nancy. Finally, after we had enjoyed a glorious afternoon in the sunshine, the flaps at the front of the tent parted and out strode the three heroes, Nancy, Luis and Richard, proudly bearing their showstopper bakes. Luis had a model of a coalmine with winding gear whilst Richard and Nancy had model windmills. All three amazing works of art in cake, pastry and sugar work. There appeared to be little to choose between the three of them. Paul and Mary appeared along with Mel and Sue and they announced the winner. They presented Nancy with a cake stand and a bunch of flowers. Some had thought that perhaps Richard would be the winner, as he had been voted Star Baker five times. However, as Mr Hollywood always said it is how one performs on the day that counts and Nancy had excelled herself with the Technical bake and perhaps her Showstopper was just a wee bit more outstanding than the other two.

Truth be known, any one of the three was capable of winning the Bakeoff but to quote Paul, "The fact that you have made it to the tent proves that all twelve of you are winners". I think that is the attitude taken by all twelve of the bakers, as we have remained the best of friends to this day. We all thought it was just a pity that we could not have been together for all ten weeks of the Bakeoff, but I am afraid one of us had to go each week, always a sad occasion but especially in Week Five!

II The Extra Slice

The GBBO Series 5 2014 saw the introduction of a new half hour programme on BBC2, this was the Extra Slice, a comedy half hour hosted by the sharp mind and brilliant wit of comedienne, and all-round presenter, Jo Brand. Accompanying Jo each week were a panel of three celebrities, carefully selected by Love Productions for their charm, wit and baking knowledge, or perhaps they were just short of a bob or two that week. The Bakeoff contestant who had been eliminated that week starred alongside Jo for the thirty minutes of jollity. Hats off to my friend Claire who was the first of us to undergo this trial; I watched the show and thought she handled herself brilliantly. The recording of the show took place at a television studio in London in front of an audience of around two hundred souls. Whoever was the subject of the programme in that particular week was allowed to bring ten friends along and no expense was spared in getting the contestant to the studio, including hotel accommodation and provision of a chauffeur driven limo, one did feel important for that day.

I was very pleased to be appearing alongside the panel selected for my own Extra Slice after Week Five of the Bakeoff. None other than the well-known Michelin Starred Chef, Michel Roux, joined by former budding rock star, postman and Labour Cabinet Minister The Rt.Hon. Alan

Johnson MP; and adding her wit, beauty and charm was comedienne Shappi Khorsandi, an impressive panel by anyone's standards. I was requested to bring a bake along to the show, one that was relevant to the Bakeoff theme in the week of my elimination. As my week was Pie Week - incidentally a week in which I thought I would excel and even had the temerity to think along the lines of "Star Baker" – I brought along a Chicken, Mushroom & Tarragon Pie in rough puff pastry. This was warmed up and presented to the panel and I was particularly proud of the fact that Michel thought it an excellent pie. It was remarkable that this pie had survived the journey by air from Aberdeen, as I had to put it in with our hold luggage lest security prevented on board carriage.

The Mem Sahib and myself had flown from Dyce Aerodrome in Aberdeen to Heathrow where we were whisked off to a hotel on the Southbank to spend the night before being collected by a further limo and taken to the studio at 10am the following morning. We spent virtually the whole day in the green room at the studio before being taken to the makeup department where a nice young lady brushed powder over my shiny bits and then I was off into the studio. Iris, Corinne and Louise were already in the audience as was Sonya and Martin Arnell (Sonya as an ex manager of mine along with my good friend Carol Watt had provided an initial reference for Love Productions when I applied for the Bakeoff). In addition, present in the audience were a few of Corinne and Louise's friends who came along to make up my ten permitted guests.

Until this moment, I had adopted a casual attitude toward cameras, microphones and meeting well-known celebrities and thought I was ready for anything. What I was not prepared for was the thunderous roar of applause from the two hundred or so people in the audience when I walked on to the set and met Jo and the panel. One could easily get used to this adulation and I now had some understanding of why ageing actors, singers and celebrities continue working way beyond the age when they should be sitting at home with pipe and slippers and as my Dad used to say "Marking time for the boneyard".

The audience appeared to enjoy the spectacle and it seemed to be all over very quickly although Mrs C said she had been sitting there for two hours. Finally, they presented me with a cake having a model of myself and Sue Perkins on the top. Complete with a bottle of champagne I departed the stage, later meeting up with the girls, Sonia, Martin and Mrs C before heading off for a meal and back to the hotel. We were taken once more by limo to Heathrow before flying back to Aberdeen and home once more. I had to leave the champagne with Corinne and Louise who said they would keep it for a special occasion, which I gather is Louise's graduation from the O.U. in 2016.

III The Final Extra Slice

Not long after our wonderful day out at the Bakeoff Final, we had the additional thrill of all of us Bakers meeting up again for the Extra Slice Final. We were all to be there at Pinewood Studios and each of us was transported to the hotel near Pinewood where we met up for dinner in the evening. All that is except the winner and two finalists, Nancy, Luis and Richard, who were hidden away from us in a separate hotel. It was a great pity that we could not have all been reunited but nonetheless we had a splendid evening with an excellent meal and no shortage of liquid refreshment. Our evening lasted until the next morning and it was not until the early hours that everyone managed to climb aboard their hammocks.

Unlike our stay at the Elcot Park Mercure we had a splendid breakfast before being transported to Pinewood Studios where the Final Extra Slice was to be filmed, but this time we had Paul and Mary as the celebrity guests on the panel along with a comic singer whose name escapes me. Jo Brand was in the chair as normal, the only missing personalities were Mel and Sue, and I felt that if they had been there, it would have been the icing on the cake. Nevertheless, we had a great afternoon and once Richard and Luis had made their stage appearances, followed by our winning Nancy, we managed to have a group photograph taken. Regrettably, the only member missing was Nancy who had been spirited away for a photography session elsewhere. I managed to get a Bakeoff Book signed by everyone, including Mary and Paul but as I have mentioned we did not have Mel and Sue there for the picture.

Final Extra Slice, the assembled Bakers + Mary & Paul, you can just see that Richard still has the pencil behind his lug.

Farthing Biscuits

My final recipe is for the famous Farthing Biscuits, the ones that I made in Week Two of the Bakeoff and for these I was honoured to receive the Hollywood Handshake.

Farthings, AKA Butter Biscuits or Tea Biscuits

FARTHINGS RECIPE

8oz plain flour

8oz self-raising flour

3oz lard

3oz butter

1 teaspoon salt

1 teaspoon sugar

cold water to make a firm dough

Mix dry ingredients and rub in butter & lard. Mix in just enough water to make a stiff dough. Roll out thinly to just less than thickness of a one pound coin & pr!ck all over.

Arrange the biscuits on a baking tray lined with baking parchment or a baking mesh if you have one. Traditionally, these were baked on a wire mesh tray and using a baking mesh leaves a nice imprint on the bottom of the biscuit.

Bake 15 minutes at 180 degrees C. Do not allow to turn brown.

These will keep for weeks in a sealed container and are excellent spread with butter or with any cheese.

CHAPTER NINETEEN

Frequently Asked Questions

I was just beginning to congratulate myself on almost finishing this book when I thought, what if I have not covered most things people want to know about the Bakeoff. I decided then to add this additional wee bit on F.A.Q's or frequently asked questions.

I have made a short list of some of the questions I have been asked during the past two years but if somehow you feel I have not addressed your particular query, please contact me via my website http://www.normancalder.com with your question and I will be more than happy to give you an answer if I can.

What is your opinion of the judges, Paul and Mary?

The judges have a difficult job in that they have to send someone home every week; even if everyone appears equal, they still need to find a reason to eliminate someone. Mary is nothing less than a warm and wonderful human being and even if she has reason to criticise some aspect of your baking, she will always conclude with a positive comment regarding some aspect which she feels you have made a decent job of. Paul is a very talented baker and the editing process used on the GBBO may sometimes make him appear a touch forthright. However, I would say that Paul is the sort of bloke you would be happy having a pint with at your local. His honesty needs to be admired; if you mess it up, he will let you know.

What happens to all the goodies baked by the contestants?

Once the session is complete the contestants disappear to have coffee in the green room, on return there is generally nothing left as it will have been consumed by the crew (there are over fifty of them in the tent), if your bakes are untouched – worry.

Did you have to spend your own money during the Bakeoff?

Just the expenses for the first and second auditions, although if you are travelling a long distance you may get assistance with travel expenses for the second audition. Once you are chosen to participate in the Bakeoff you are given an allowance for each week you are in, to cover the cost of ingredients used in practice. If you are fortunate enough to make it through to the end, you should be in receipt of around £500. Once you are selected, all travel and hotel bills are settled by Love Productions. Theoretically, you should not be out of pocket but I did splash out on a KitchenAid stand mixer and an ice cream maker.

Are contestants paid a fee by Love productions?

No fee is payable for the contestants appearance in the Bakeoff. Everyone else gets a fee, according to press reports in 2015, the fee for the top talent was £500,000 each with Mel and Sue each receiving around £100,000. Due to the outstanding success of Bakeoff 2015, it has been reported that the two Stars of the Bakeoff will get an additional £100,000 each for their part in the 2016 production. The winner of Bakeoff gets a bouquet and a cake stand.

What did you like most about the Bakeoff?

I found the entire experience very rejuvenating and enjoyed every minute of it. The average human being considers himself very lucky to be able to count his friends using all the fingers of one hand. I now need both my hands plus my left foot. All of us from Series Five continue to correspond on a daily basis using the mobile telephone application, WhatsApp. I guess then that I appreciate the new friendships more than anything else. It will not surprise you to learn that we, the Series Five contestants, think we were the best ever!

How many hours did you have to spend each day at Welford Park?

The first day of each weekend's filming was always the longest; we would be picked up from the hotel at 6:20am and sometimes not return to the hotel until 9pm. The first day of the first week was the most demanding, we had lunch at 4pm. The second day was usually much shorter as the contestants had to travel home so it was generally all over by 6pm. For myself it did not matter as we always finished too late for me to catch the last flight, so had to stay an extra night in the hotel.

Is there anything you would change about the Bakeoff?

We were collected from the hotel at 6:20am only to have to sit around for hours. I would suggest they collect the contestants at 9am at the earliest – after they have eaten a decent breakfast.

Why do you think the Bakeoff is so successful?

I think its continuing success is to do with the fact that we are all amateurs and never appear overly competitive. If this quality can be maintained, I believe that the Bakeoff will continue to appeal to many. When you watch the Bakeoff, you should be saying to yourself that you could do as well if not better. I would not like to see the programme becoming too professional. I consider my own attitude to the competition to be the most rewarding; do not take it too seriously. Although you may well publish a book or if you're lucky, get paid for appearances after the Bake-off, do not go into it with this commercial thought in your head.

Did you feel nervous in the tent?

Not at all, what makes it easy for the contestant is the fact that all ingredients are prepared for you, checked against your proposed recipe and placed on your bench. Any bowls, utensils etc., which you use, are whisked away for washing. There are plenty of spare utensils available and if you require a fresh bowl or utensil, you just go pick one up. The crew in the tent also help enormously and if you need anything at all, they will procure whatever it is in an instant. So all you have to do is bake, maybe smile for the camera now and again, have a
laugh with Mel and Sue and be nice to Paul and Mary.

Any downsides to making the programme?

The only part most of us found annoying was the continual "interview" process. Around three times a day you would be asked to go with a producer, cameraman and sound engineer to a location behind a tree, on a bridge or somewhere else remote from the tent, there to undergo an interview process. The primary object of this exercise was to provide some film footage to add to the edited programme, bits about how you got on that day etc. They also took the op-portunity in my case to emphasise at least twice a day that my bakes were very plain and sim-ple and when was I going to "up my game". In truth I was really getting a bit fed up with that and I fell into their trap, I think, and that's why I changed my pie recipes and used the lavender – my mistake.

Did your life change post Bakeoff?

I did get recognised by strangers when out and about but that was easy to cope with as they were all very nice and just wanted a "selfie" or sometimes an autograph. I have been pestered by "Hello" magazine but so far have managed to shake them off. Since the Bakeoff, life in gen-eral has been busier, not a bad thing.

Did you do a lot of practice for the Bakeoff?

Obviously not enough but I did a bit, if whatever I was test baking turned out OK I just did it the once.

Do you still bake at home?

Yes indeed, in fact more frequently and with a touch more variety than I did before my Bakeoff appearance. I must say, however, that like most things I do, I am beginning to, not so much tire of baking, but I am at that stage where I am looking for something else to do. Although I can do quite a lot and am always keen on something new, I have never been very good at anything. Every day of my life, I have continued to know less and less about more and more. Unlike the expert who every day knows more and more about less and less. The expert will eventually end up knowing everything about nothing; myself, I will end up knowing nothing about everything. A slight exaggeration perhaps but that kinda sums up what I am about.

What are your plans for the future?

If I am spared and well I will reach the age of sixty-nine in June 2016, so I think that planning too much for the future would challenge the Giftie himself. I have no "bucket list" to speak of so would just like to continue enjoying good health, good company and good food. Oh!, and the occasional ~~glass~~ bottle of Chateau Neuf Du Pape.

Who is your favourite chef/baker on television?

I have watched them all, from Fanny and Johnny Craddock, through The Galloping Gourmet and Delia Smith to James Martin and the Hairy Bikers, but my favourite remains Keith Floyd. As well as a fantastic chef, Keith was a great entertainer and I will always be grateful for his advice on how to cook with wine – you drink most of it!.

Have you made any financial gain as a result of your Bakeoff appearance?

Many of the appearances I have been invited to make have been with the purpose of helping charitable organisations, with one or two exceptions where I have received a fee and expenses. Overall, I would say that the one has balanced out the other. Although there has been little financial gain, I have profited immensely from the experience and made many new friends. There is little more one can ask of life. Just as Shakespeare has a quotation for most occasions, so in Scotland Robert Burns provides thoughtful words for guidance in life. A favourite of my Uncle, **Norman Byron Calder**, was the following by Robert Burns........

from "Here's to thy health my bonnie lass".........

I ken they scorn my low estate,
But that does never grieve me;
For I'm as free as any he,
Sma' siller will relieve me.
I'll count my health my greatest wealth
Sae lang as I'll enjoy it:
I'll fear nae scant, I'll bode nae want
As lang's I get employment.

Epilogue

That was it Dear Reader, a concise account of my Bakeoff experience along with a wee bit regarding the early part of my life. If this short account is well received, I may continue the dialogue in further essays. Meantime, I would like to thank you for taking the time to read this far, and trust that you have enjoyed the experience as much as I appreciated being part of the Bakeoff Series 5 2014. Grateful thanks to Carol Watt and Sonia Ingleton for providing me with a reference for Love Productions. Many thanks also to Murray Grindon, our Bakeoff chaperone, and to my Bakeoff colleagues for becoming good friends. Finally, thanks to all at Love Productions, Mary, Paul, Mel and Sue for the experience of a lifetime!

If after reading this you think you would like to apply for the Bakeoff at any time and would like some advice, please feel free to contact me via my website http://www.normancalder.com and I will be delighted to be of assistance. Just remember if you are looking for advice always ask a failure as he will already have done all the wrong things.

Cheerio for now,

Norman

Made in the USA
Middletown, DE
24 October 2020